Nigel Barley

NATIVE LAND

VIKING

VIKING

Published by the Penguin Group
27 Wrights Lane, London W8 5TZ, England
Viking Penguin Inc., 40 West 23rd Street, New York, New York 10010, USA
Penguin Books Australia Ltd, Ringwood, Victoria, Australia
Penguin Books Canada Ltd, 2801 John Street, Markham, Ontario, Canada L3R 1B4
Penguin Books (NZ) Ltd, 182–190 Wairau Road, Auckland 10, New Zealand

Penguin Books Ltd, Registered Offices: Harmondsworth, Middlesex, England

First published 1989
10 9 8 7 6 5 4 3 2 1

Printed in Great Britain by Richard Clay Ltd, Bungay, Suffolk
Typeset in 10/13 pt Lasercomp Photina

A CIP catalogue record for this book is available from the British Library

ISBN 0-670-83039-9

Contents

Acknowledgements
Photographic credits

For permission to use copyright material, grateful acknowledgement is made to the following: The Johns Hopkins University Press for the excerpt from *Western Attitudes Towards Death From the Middle Ages to the Present* by Philippe Aries: B. T. Batsford Ltd for the excerpt from *Victorian Things* by Asa Briggs; Methuen London for the lines from 'The Stately Homes of England' by Noel Coward, published in *The Lyrics of Noel Coward*; Presses Universitaries de France for the excerpt from *Sociologie et Anthropologie* by Marcel Mauss; the American Anthropological Association for the excerpt from 'Body Ritual Among the Nacirema' by Horace Miner; The Peters Fraser and Dunlop Group Ltd for the excerpt from *Labels* by Evelyn Waugh.

Photographic credits

TVS, page 10; Shahid Rasul/Art Directors, page 38; Topham, page 60; Colin Molyneux/The Image Bank, page 84; Alain le Garsmeur/Impact Photos, page 118; Barnaby's, page 140.

Introduction

*When you marry, marry a lady anthropologist. She
will have been trained for years never to interrupt you
and to say only just enough to keep you talking.*
[Advice of an eminent Finnish anthropologist.]

This book follows on from, and covers much of the
same ground as, a six-part television documentary of the same
name screened by Channel 4. However, books and television
make quite different demands on the writer. The former depend
primarily upon the word, the latter upon the image, so that a
book offers much greater opportunities to analyse and explain
rather than to encapsulate meaning in a striking picture.

The television series dealt with a journey of discovery to try to
pin down some general idea of the contemporary English identity.
Its inspiration lay in the feeling of alienation that overwhelms
anyone returning from living abroad for any considerable period
who feels required to give some account of his own culture.
Within the confines of six half-hour programmes it is impossible
to give an exhaustive profile of the English identity. One must of
necessity be thematic and idiosyncratic.

Anthropologists are far from being a homogenous bunch and
vary widely in both methods and aims. They are students of
society and culture, but are unable to agree on what precise
meaning is to be given to either of these words. Some speak in

terms of offering descriptions, others of analyses. The word 'explanation' is heard less and less. Like prophets of all description, anthropologists are not without honour save in their own country. Traditionally, they have worked in distant lands, studying peoples who are representative of all that we hold to be alien and 'other'. When they *have* worked within the United Kingdom, they have tended to concern themselves with the Celtic fringe, gypsies, disadvantaged groups – everyone, in fact, but the mainstream English, however we define them. It might be argued that it is the distinction between sociologists (who work 'at home') and anthropologists (who work 'abroad') that marks and maintains the line between the two great groupings of our world – people who are held to be like us and those who are distinctively different. It is becoming increasingly difficult to treat such a line seriously.

According to the introductory lectures given to generations of first-year students, anthropologists concern themselves with small, traditional, face-to-face communities. Usually, these are described as 'non-literate' – more optimistically as 'pre-literate'. Yet we live in a world where the peoples of anthropological literature are acquiring literacy while the younger generation of our own culture seems to be discarding it. Size of population itself is no guarantee of anything. We are aware, in what is clearly the ethnographic territory of Africa and Asia, of traditional peoples numbering several millions, while close-up, the mass groupings of the West decompose themselves into the small communities of work and home inside which we, too, interact on a one-to-one basis. There is thus every reason to be suspicious of the line between those who study their own culture and those who work outside it. It is all too easy for such a division to become a covert means of asserting our own inherent superiority or rationality, or of maintaining myths and preconceptions about the world and our own privileged place in it.

But for the ethnographer there are a number of very real differences between working in the African bush and the urban wastes of England. It is one of the curious paradoxes of anthropology that to become an 'expert' on a particular culture it is first necessary to be completely ignorant of it – to be a total foreigner. Why should this be so? The conventional answer is that it is only the encounter with the alien that renders culture visible at all. Our own culture is like our own nose. We do not see it because it is in front of our very eyes and we are accustomed to look straight through it to see the world. Indeed, if we see it at all, we see it as *part* of the world. The culture of others, like the noses on *their* faces, is readily apparent and lends itself to detached and protracted study and comparison.

The anthropologist working at home is thus in a curious position and may either be forced to engage in many awkward contortions to see himself or, better, try to glimpse his own image in the mirror of the 'other' cultures that he has studied over the years. It is this tension between being simultaneously inside and outside the culture on which he works that generates both the strengths and the weaknesses of the anthropologist's position, for it is necessarily one of comparison, yet one of informed subjectivity. It is one of the basic beliefs of anthropology that cultures must be studied in their own terms through the categories of their members. Yet for the anthropologist to be both native informant and analyst raises all manner of difficulties about how we should view the relation between the native's account of his culture and the investigator's. This is the principal reason for recruiting an English native informant, Jim Batchelor.

A word on method. Anthropologists rarely work with questionnaires and statistics. They are more concerned with 'intersubjective meanings', the ideas by which people make sense of their lives. Thus, for the anthropologist, history is less 'what really happened' than 'what people remember'. Culture is seen as a little like a language. No two people may speak exactly alike, yet there is still a a sense in which all native speakers speak 'the same' language and, indeed, have to in order to be able to communicate. Such ideas do not lend themselves to easy measurement, but are best studied through the technique of 'participant observation', a complex name for a simple thing. It means taking part in everyday activities, as much as possible, like a native and preferably over a long period. This was one of the areas where making a television programme differed most from being an anthropologist in the field. The anthropologist tries to disturb local activities as little as he or she can, to pass, as far as possible, unnoticed. This is the sense of the words of the Finnish ethnographer quoted at the beginning of the chapter. Clearly, to arrive with a film crew and a whole load of intrusive equipment for a matter of hours or days violates many of the rules of anthropological method. Yet it is not without advantages.

There are many native voices in these pages, the many people we talked to both informally and in interviews on camera. Often they are quoted at length. It is a rare luxury to be able to make video recordings of your informants! Usually, they are transcribed and roughly translated in all manner of mutilated and makeshift forms in the ethnographer's tattered notebooks. Yet remarks on camera are very much public statements, which may have to be defended like the speeches of politicians. The ethnographer often requires access to the private and even the unconscious. Cameras, curiously, may help to elicit the most private thoughts and interpretations. When they are switched off, they act as guarantors of immediate intimacy. As they are packed away, people may well pass automatically from a wholly conventional expression of what they feel they *ought* to think to a frank statement of what they *do* think.

Another major difference of working 'at home' lies in the power relations between anthropologist and people worked on. It is relatively easy for the anthropologist of distant places to hijack the identity and culture of those he studies. Locals are rarely able to tell him that his interpretations are wrong and that they know better. Such is not the case when working on your own culture. Many have found the programme *Native Land* provocative of both thought and comment.

4

The Field Assistant

In anthropological books there is always a shadowy and largely unacknowledged figure that lurks behind the writer, like the wife of a famous man – the field assistant. The anthropologist usually works on a group whose language and rules of interaction are unfamiliar to him. In the early stages he is unable to make himself understood or risk contact with others except through his assistant, who guides him and apologizes for his gaucheries to his hosts. The duties of a field assistant are many and ill-defined. In our own culture they are most closely paralleled by those of a nanny.

In the present case the field assistant was our Cockney driver, Jim Batchelor, a man of forthright speech, clear opinions and impeccably English identity. It is always to the field assistant that the anthropologist turns initially for the native view. Jim's views were often different from my own in that he was working entirely within his own culture while I, as ethnographer, was already half an alien. Thus at the wedding that formed the basis of the first programme he was able to give an enormous amount of information about the technicalities of weddings, but never bothered to mention that it is only persons of opposite sexes who may marry each other and then only one at a time. For Jim, these are rules so obvious that he would regard them as inevitable and universal. An anthropologist knows that they are not.

Often we would be working away from the urban environment, where Jim feels most at ease. In such situations he, too, would feel alienated. Significantly, however, he would continue to interpret the behaviour of those around him by his own standards, regarding it as 'odd', 'weird' or even 'unBritish'.

It is inevitable that in the course of assisting the ethnographer the instinctive native vision of the assistant becomes changed.

5

There is a sense in which all anthropologists are polluting the stream they drink from. Thus, to ask the average English person, 'How do you think about your body?' is an unanswerable and ridiculous question, rather like asking 'What is the sex of roast beef?' To ask an ethnographic informant the same question is perfectly reasonable, since he has observed the various directions from which the ethnographer has approached this question and the issues involved will be quite clear to him. Thus every investigator breeds the informants who give him the sort of answers he is looking for.

Variation

Anthropologists, unlike sociologists, have never been much concerned to account for variation within the patterns of behaviour of a single culture. They paint with a broad brush to give a large-scale map. Also, it has often been assumed that traditional cultures are fundamentally different in type from our own 'complex' culture – that they permit of less variation and are more homogenous. Any anthropologist in the field knows that the individual people he has to deal with may not resemble, in any easy way, the abstractions and generalizations of the text-books. Not being interested in individual biography, however, he continues to generalize. He does so in the belief that generalizations may tell little lies but, it is to be hoped, in the service of a greater truth.

In English culture the natives have developed their own specialists, sociologists, who teach them to explain variation amongst themselves in terms of region, age and class. Class is an interesting native concept that has been adopted, quite unreasonably, for cross-cultural use by sociologists, struggling with desperate dedication to bring it in line with a now discarded notion of science, one that relates it to universality and reducibility to statistical data. Little wonder, then, that the 'class' of sociologists bears little relation to native intuitions. This is emphatically *not* yet another book about the English class system; indeed, class is largely irrelevant to it.

The English, the British and the Rest

Nowadays ethnic terms are treated at arm's length. They are contentious and must be safely hedged round with deferential preamble or locked within the safety of inverted commas. It is provocative to use the term 'English' to include Scots, Welsh and other peoples of the UK. The correct term, we are told, is 'British'. The current usage of many residents of the UK and most of the world contradicts this. 'English' is commonly used at two different levels, the first contrasting the British with the rest of the world, the second contrasting the English with the other constituent peoples of the UK. Thus informants would regularly produce statements such as, 'To be British you have to be born in England . . .' It is significant of changes in our views of national identity that this usage is historically justified but currently contentious. 'Englishness' is the term *against which* many of the component peoples of the UK define their own identities. A plea for linguistic parity is part of a plea for parity of status.

The programmes on which this book is based sought to deal only with the English identity and therefore deliberately avoided the problems of regionalism. However, because 'English' is a demotic synonym for 'British', many of the statements recorded here will apply equally well to other component peoples of the UK. On the other hand, some English informants when questioned about English matters, replied in terms of 'the British'.

Because of this, attempts to focus *only* on the English may appear to imply a furious nationalistic fervour that prejudices the identities of other parts of the UK, dismissing them as of secondary importance. This was not the intention, yet clearly *does* reflect an interesting fact about the English identity and its curiously problematic status.

1 Contemporary English Myths

The detestation of 'quaintness' and 'picturesque bits'
which is felt by every decently constituted Englishman
is, after all, a very insular prejudice. It has developed
naturally in self-defence against arts and crafts, and the
preservation of rural England and the preservation of
ancient monuments, and the transplantation of Tudor
cottages, and the collection of pewter and old oak and
the reformed public house, and Ye Olde Inne.

Evelyn Waugh,
Labels

THE FIRST THING that strikes one on returning to English cities from just about anywhere apart from Eastern Europe is that people look so miserable. There could be any number of explanations for this but some leap readily to mind:

1 The English expression of facial repose coincidentally looks like that of glum discontent in other cultures. The depressed souls of English cities are simply 'switched off'.
2 The English emotional thermostat is in some sense set lower, so that the natives are either less emotional or at least less demonstrative.
3 Facial expressions are not universal but are learnt as part of culture. Therefore an outsider cannot make inferences from facial expressions to internal states. The English idiom is simply different.
4 The English *are* glum, perhaps for some justifiable reason.

There is nothing more difficult in other cultures than trying to find out how other people *feel*. There is no way of knowing whether words for emotions can be accurately equated. One cannot simply look at what people *do*. In some cultures it is not uncommon to cry from joy or to sing from grief. This is one clear area where the native ethnographer is at a considerable advantage. For once, he does not need to worry about language. He merely assumes the common meaning of facial expressions *within* his own culture.

Even the most superficial ethnographic research indicates that all the above possibilities are probably true to some degree. Informants will be found who assent to one or more quite readily. Yet the striking thing is that many of the natives, when questioned, do not even *expect* to be happy. They point to the hectic lives they lead, their work or its absence, commuting, the struggle to make ends meet; in short, they regard their urban existence as 'unnatural'. There is much talk of 'pressure' and 'stress'. Medical experts regularly produce new evidence of the consequences of our unnatural way of living: fatigue, impotence, cancer. It seems clear that they must be carrying some model of 'natural' life around in their heads.

The phenomenon is quite surprising. Most traditional peoples seem to regard the way they live as both splendidly 'natural' and inevitable. They do the things they do because this is the only reasonable way things could possibly be done. For English city dwellers, however, natural life seems to be situated not within their own life-style at all. It is to be found in two other places:

> 1 outside our culture entirely, in the zones where anthropology has free reign and a fantasy paradise may be located;
> 2 in the country.

The country is not just a place, it is a value, something self-evidently good in itself. The status of the English countryside as a value is clear from the determination of many to be there whenever they are not bound up with work in the city. Whole villages are now weekend retreats or retirement ghettos. People who have been born in towns nevertheless speak of themselves as 'getting back' to the country. Although the English countryside is almost entirely man-made, its admirers insist on seeing it as completely 'natural'.

The contemporary mark that something is of value is that it is regarded as under threat. It will then be sure to have its own preservation society, which protects it and propagandizes on its behalf. The English countryside has spawned many of these. It is another mark of such basic values that informants are notoriously incapable of saying precisely *why* such things are important. To ask why the countryside is important is thus to seem deliberately obtuse. It is like asking why one would not wish to be eaten by a shark.

The countryside as a value represents a 'natural' way of life that has been lost. As such, to go to the country is seen as going back in time, to regain one's roots in myth. English assumptions about such things are doggedly evolutionist. Any anthropologist knows that, outside his own trade, people will view time spent in an African village as a return to a 'stage of development' that we have now left behind. This encompasses not merely technology but also social relations and human abilities.

But closer examination shows that we are in the presence of not one, but two, clusters of mythic ideas. While these are totally opposed, an informant may well pass between them effortlessly, switching back and forth at will. Evelyn Waugh, quoted at the beginning of this chapter, was vividly aware that every myth generates its opposite in some inevitable dialectic.

The first world view is basically romantic. It values the old, the traditional, the 'natural'. Its favoured material objects are antique or hand-crafted as opposed to machine-made. Things should not be designed; they should grow almost organically over the years and be rooted in a way of life. Their justification is, then, not rationality, but history. It is said, with some justification, that an English factory owner who wishes to impress you is more likly to show you an ancient machine left over from his grandfather's era than his brand-new one. The shrines of this myth are, of course, museums and ancient monuments. Since the English now regard their past as a place they wish to go to, these enter into the notion of England as a theme park.

The second myth is modernist and technological. It values the newest and the latest, anything that can be regarded as an application of design principles. Its objects are hard-edged and machine-made with no sign of human agency or the flaws of age. Such a myth has its shrines, Cape Canaveral and Beaubourg for example, but it has no fixed location to call its own except in the works of science fiction that project it on to an unformed future.

English culture draws heavily on both. Indeed, both may be invoked by the same person with reference to the same object.

Thus, to drive a vintage car or the very latest model with all the extras will make one a figure of envy. To drive last year's model makes one simply prosaic.

No contradiction is seen in such myth-hopping. Myths are not necessarily in competition with each other nor are they opposed to that which is true. They may well be true. Truth, however, is largely irrelevant to them since they merely organize data without external comparisons. But these myths form the background to the first chapter and will be picked up elsewhere in the book.

A Country Wedding

A wedding is a time when social relations are displayed on the ground like a map. As the major ritual event left in contemporary life, a wedding is a time when relationships are redefined and made public. They are an excellent way of getting to grips with the social life of country people. We visited the village of Smallwood in Cheshire to look at one.

Smallwood is a curious village in that it seems to lack a centre. Historically, this is explicable, as there never was a central estate around which a core would have formed, the area being composed of small freeholdings. Few exceed 200 acres. Following recent decisions made by the EEC, dairy herding is now greatly reduced and most farms are a mixture of arable and fatstock (whereby calves are bought in, fattened and resold for slaughter). The history of the area is seen as justifying a sturdy, personal self-reliance, yet a town-dweller is immediately struck by a strong sense of continuity and community. In the course of our filming, this became ever more evident. The page at the wedding was the son of the butcher we met at the slaughterhouse. The organist turned out to be the farmer we first wanted to talk to about showjumping. The same names that came up in interviews – Ford, Jepson, Bracegirdle – were on the gravestones outside the church where the wedding was to be held. It was typical that as we were filming at the church, ladies we had filmed at the Women's Institute walked into frame and began to put flowers on the graves. Jim Batchelor immediately identified this as like the old East End, now gone. For him, going to the country was time travel.

The lay-out of the village reflects the traditional associations that have organized public life. The school stands right next to the church. The village hall is opposite. There are four pubs in Smallwood. Most are 'road-houses', drawing passing trade from the main roads on which they are situated. More difficult to find, more clearly a 'local', is the Blue Bell.

The Pub

In many societies, there is a place that constitutes a sort of neutral ground where people can meet in a public place without the strains that come from being on someone else's home ground. In West Africa this is the space under the village's meeting tree. In England it is the pub. Its full title of public *house* is significant. Although such places seem immediately natural and non-problematic to those of English culture, an enormous amount of cultural information has to be known in order to behave properly in such a setting.

Pubs are prime territory for the ethnographer and it is here that we began in Smallwood. Here people are at their ease and willing to talk. Often they will discuss and digest matters of recognized importance without prompting or intervention. The public house also indicates the importance of the private house, with its associated notions of privacy. This we shall look at in a later chapter.

Although a public space, a pub is not without internal divisions. It is fertile ground for observing the ways the English use objects and the patterns of their exchange both to build walls and create bridges. The Blue Bell at Smallwood has a number of small bars and each has a different clientele.

> *Bob Slack (landlord):* You get your regulars in the tap-room bar. The one next door . . . not the very end one, that's the younger people. That's where they tend to go, in there. Your regulars in that bar, and this bar has a different type of regular. Business people in here and the working lads in there and then the people that come in the lounge are usually, well, some regulars but those just visiting, yes.
> *Nigel Barley:* But you don't direct people? They just know?
> *Bob:* No. It just seems to happen like that and always has done.

The English are automatically sorting themselves out into distinctive categories, presumably shared by insiders and outsiders alike, according to all manner of subtle cues: hard chairs versus soft, presence or absence of a fireplace, flowers on the tables, and so on.

It is within the bars that groups form for the exchange of drinks, persons taking turns to order a 'round'. This social aspect of drinking is such a powerful element that some English students have regarded solitary drinking as automatically a sign of impending alcoholism. Inclusion in, or exclusion from, the round is a mark of the offering, or withholding, of a social relationship. To dodge one's round, to refuse an offered drink without good reason, to 'forget' someone – all constitute eloquent statements about oneself in a public arena where judgements are made about the sort of person you are and where you stand in the community. Needless to say, drinks have to be appropriate to persons and in an English pub a complex grammar distinguishes between male and female drinks. One may thus be asked whether a half-pint of beer is for male or female consumption since this governs what sort of glass it has to be put in.

It is often here that first decisions are made about applications for 'insider' status. Like many English villages, Smallwood seems to operate a distinction between insider and outsider. People born into the village are insiders on grounds of history and residence. Others have to earn acceptance. Several stressed the importance of the pub for gaining admission to the village.

Keith Woolley, for example, is a recent arrival. Together with his wife, Michelle, he has taken over the village store. Previously, both had white-collar jobs in industry but wanted to 'get back' to the country. Running the store involves a good deal of travel to the more remote farms to deliver goods, and Keith finds himself engaged in many informal acts of good neighbouring, such as cutting wood for old ladies. Yet it is the pub that seems central to integration within the village.

> *NB:* So how did you set about trying to get into the
> community and what's the focus of it for you?
> *Keith:* Maybe the pub.
> *NB:* The pubs are important?
> *Keith:* Well, it is to me. It matters much to me. I like a drink,
> so I like to nip out there and have a pint and a chat to people.

We should note that Keith, unlike his interviewer, thinks in terms of only *one* pub. Smallwood people give loyalty to a single pub and questions may be asked if the regular of one pub is seen drinking elsewhere.

The pub, of course, is more than a place to drink. In Smallwood it runs a football team, golf society, an offshore sailing club. Indeed, drinking is not accounted a major activity in the pub.

> *Bob:* . . . I've heard people say in here that they haven't had
> a beer at home since Christmas. They wouldn't dream of
> having a drink. They just turn out half an hour before
> closing time and have a couple of pints and a chat, and
> they'd rather do that than sit in on a winter's night.

The Blue Bell is also the meeting place for the Young Farmers, a self-explanatory group, who meet every Monday to play dominoes, the married ones being licensed to come without their wives. It is here that we meet the groom of our impending wedding. The all-male company and an imminent wedding transform the occasion into a reduced version of the stag night that had already occurred.

The Family

Peter Barlow is 29 years old and is marrying Janet Moss, 24, the daughter of his employer of ten years' standing, after a two-year engagement. It is to be a big church wedding with a large reception held in a marquee at the bride's parents' farm. No expense has been spared. The couple are suitably shy. The dominant figure is clearly the bride's father, Philip Moss.

Philip, as well as running a small farm, owns a successful business dealing in farm machinery and machine parts. He is extrovert and articulate. When speaking of him in the village, people often grin and describe him as a 'bit of a lad' or some such. Their attitude seems a mixture of disapproval of someone who upsets traditional methods and admiration for his material success and winning ways. Philip makes it clear that he regards the expenditure on the wedding as a public statement of the value he sets on his daughter, a modern equivalent of the dowry.

> *Philip:* Some might consider it a waste of money. I think
> that, hopefully, they don't get married twice and I think
> that it isn't a waste of money in that sense. I think you can
> go too far, obviously, and then it becomes a little bit of a
> bore financially, but if the daughter isn't worth a good
> wedding, then . . .

In fact, the reference to getting married twice is quite significant. Peter, the groom, *has* been married before and is divorced. Nevertheless a church wedding has been agreed, the service to be performed by a former vicar of the local church and a friend of the family.

Peter works with Philip in the machinery business and is a director of the firm. This is their principal source of income, yet both he and his employer insist that they are *really* farmers.

Philip: I farm because I'm initially a farmer, a farmer's son born and bred, and I like it – and there's nothing nicer, you know, at the end of the day when the telephone has been ringing fifty or sixty times, than to pick a stick up and go and walk round the cattle . . . The farm machinery is the business and the farming, you know, is great to get away and take it a little bit easier. It has its perils like everything else, but it's very good to get out in the land and, you know, you get a little sense of relaxation.

Peter agrees with this; indeed, he keeps a small breeding herd of prize cattle – 'for interest'.

NB: These are your cattle?
Peter: They are. This is my hobby . . .
NB: What will you do? Fatten them up and sell them off?
Peter: They're all actually in calf except for the small one.
NB: So you're actually breeding them? Why? Is there more money in that?
Peter: More enjoyment. More satisfaction on my part . . . yes, it's not the financial side – satisfaction . . . I'd like to make the farm machinery side a bit smaller. It's too big at the minute. It's a very big operation and you need to be there all the time.
NB: Don't you with farming?
Peter: You do, but farming has its busy times . . . and then it eases off and you've still plenty of jobs to do but

you're not under pressure, where the machinery business
seems to be constantly under pressure. It never lets go of you.

It could be two townsmen talking about the country and their
urge to 'return' to it. Social science tends to make you think in
terms of such opinions as being distributed in a fairly straight-
forward and predictable way, so it came as a surprise to find
such a view of things is not limited to the romantic townie.

It may be noted that the bride, Janet, also has a rather
unexpected relationship to the myth of the countryside. She runs
a market stall selling eggs, cheese and dairy produce. It is one of
the old-fashioned sort, where great blocks of cheese are sliced up
before your eyes with the economy of gesture that comes from
constant practice. But this is not *farm* produce that she makes
herself in a rustic, wood-lined kitchen; it is bought in bulk from
local, industrial creameries. Her version of appealing packaging
involves taking the plastic wrapping *off*.

Marriage

Like all institutional forms of action, marriage is a
rule-governed operation. It therefore has an internal structure
that may have little to do with the motives of individuals for
engaging in it.

The first and most obvious rule is that bride and groom should
be close but not too close. Marriage within the nuclear family is
not permitted. Traditionally, the English have married within
their own social class, age group and race. In days of religious
faith, they practised religious endogamy. In former days, given
the limited religious variation in Smallwood, this meant that
Methodists and Anglicans should not marry. I asked Joe Jepson,
a lifelong resident of Smallwood, about it.

Joe: You weren't supposed to marry really out. Religion

then was much stronger and there were lots of bits of feud going on.

Locality, too, was a limiting factor. Farmer Leonard Ford remarked:

My wife's from Nantwich, which is a village about twenty miles away from here.
NB: That's a long way, is it?
Leonard: Well, you'll find that villages are very intertwined. They only had small bikes many years ago and therefore they didn't travel very far to find their prospective wives. So to go twenty miles away was absolutely outrageous. But she's from a farming background . . .

Nowadays, of course, communications are a great deal better. People have cars and Smallwood is close to a motorway. Yet many marriages are still perceived as being between 'insiders' and such a factor is still cited with approval. Several summed this up as 'Smallwood is still Smallwood'. The general view seemed to be that this was due to the Young Farmers organization, which has brought together many young farming couples in the area and is one of the recognized ways of meeting suitable partners. The marriage of Janet and Peter is seen as one between insiders.

A wedding is analysable as a major rite of passage that shunts people from one cultural category to another. Whether civil or religious, it is a ritual that joins together, from which people emerge legally, emotionally and culturally transformed. It is common in many such rituals to separate and define the elements involved before joining them. It is this that seems to lie at the roots of the stag and hen nights.

These are special evening events where the bride and groom separately withdraw with friends of their own sex. Often this is on the day before the wedding. Traditionally, the couple should not meet again until the appointed hour at the church or register office where they are to be joined. That we are withdrawing from the everyday world into a special ritual time is marked through changes of dress and behaviour. Stag and hen nights clearly associate the participants with the animal. There will be obligatory drunkenness, obscenity, nakedness. Friends play jokes on the groom, jokes that in any other context would be viewed as definitely vicious and hurtful. The couple will be urged to 'have one last fling' before entering the constraints of matrimony. This may well be of a sexual nature. If such evenings do not end in scenes of riotous debauch that are an embarrassment to recall, they may be held to be a failure.

The day of the wedding forms a complete contrast. Bride and groom are now in formal dress and on best behaviour. This is a day when the state of the world is to be defined and held in place through the power of official papers, formal events and the images of the photographer. Whatever else happens in the church pales into insignificance beside the fact that the bride enters with her father and his surname but leaves with her husband and his.

It is a day of rich food and rich dress. Gladys Bennett, the caterer of this particular wedding, itemized the menu:

Gladys: Buck's Fizz on arrival, with a nice selection of hors d'oeuvres and that, of course, is when, we hope, everyone is going to be out there enjoying the beautiful sunshine. When they come in for the meal, they'll be greeted, of course, and we have wine to serve at the table. For starters they're having Melon Portelle, then we're having asparagus soup because Philip insists on having soup despite the weather, then we're having fresh salmon, roast beef and roast turkey, an assortment of salads, an assortment of sweets, cheese and celery, and coffee.

It is a hypercomplete meal, with serving in full of courses that would normally be regarded as alternatives only. Thus we have both soup *and* a starter. Traditionally, too, champagne is drunk – the most exuberant and wasteful form of wine – though nowadays any cheap fizzy wine that simulates champagne may be used. Here we are already dealing with symbols *of* symbols. Most of the rich clothing and the tableware are, of course, simply hired for the day.

The most mundane elements become significant and elaborated. Even the means of transporting the bride to the church and the couple away from it has to be 'special'. Usually, this is taken to mean that she will arrive in a large and decorated car, either black (formal) or white (bridal). Curiously, English weddings allow great free play with this odd element of transport in contrast to the fixity of the rest of the event and especially the service. It becomes a focus for ingenuity and inventiveness. Thus brides may well travel in hot-air balloons or on tandems. In the present case, she arrived in an open, flower-decked carriage drawn by her grandfather's prize shire horses – a gesture towards the traditional values of the country.

The clothes we wear serve to classify events. As a general rule of thumb, the greater the formality, the greater the number of clothes worn. Thus streakers, by their nakedness, are cocking a snook at the world. Weddings, on the other hand, are highly formal events and therefore characterized by the putting on of hats, gloves, waistcoats and buttonholes – elements that are largely dispensable in daily life. The contrast with hen and stag nights, characterized by great informality of dress and even nudity, could not be more marked. While the dress of the groom is fairly stereotyped, that of the bride shows a little more variation.

Informants agreed that the dress should be richly elaborate, part of the theme of the bride as 'Joan Collins for a day'. It should also be white. Its whiteness is regularly related to the sexual purity of the bride. The sexual purity of the groom is not an issue in English culture. English explicit symbolism is of a rather ponderous, ceremonial kind based on a simple notion of word meaning. The basic idea is that symbol A 'means', 'represents' or 'is' some idea B. Thus, the whiteness of the bride's dress means, represents or is purity. Other interpretations are, of course, possible. Yet the elaborate dress of the bride cannot be understood in isolation. It must be related to the food of the reception and the formal but secular stage of the wedding that follows the sacred stage in the church.

At the reception the seating distinguishes between the high table of 'the family', which now includes the closer, new relatives by marriage, and the other guests. Conversation between the family and others occurs only in the formal language of speech and toasts. Central to the entire event is the cutting of the cake.

If this event were really happening in the presence of an alien ethnographer, one, say, from Mars, he would doubtless home in on the cake as an enormously important symbol. It would be photographed, discussed and compared with other examples. He might well wish to take a collection of such cakes back to his home culture for exhibition purposes and would rage over the uncooperative unwillingness of the natives to sell them to him. (The English wedding cake has been successfully exported to many other cultures with appropriate adaptation. Thus in East Africa there may be *two* wedding cakes, one from the bride's family, the other from the groom's. In Malaysia I have seen wooden wedding cakes, the back of which could be opened to disclose cellophane-wrapped slices of fruit cake.)

While informants agree that a wedding cake is absolutely essential to the wedding, they cannot agree *why*.

> *Gladys Bennett:* [The cake is] very important, yes. It has the place of honour right in the centre of the floor. I suppose because it's always been there, hasn't it? I mean to say, it goes back for generations, doesn't it, having a wedding cake? It's part of the ritual, as I say. You *must* have a wedding cake . . . The first thing the women will do tomorrow when

they get in the marquee will [be to] go to look at the
wedding cake. All the ladies. The men won't bother of
course. They'll be busy having a drink.
NB: And they'll all pass judgement?
Gladys: Oh yes, they'll all pass comment. Yes, definitely.

One popular native interpretation was that the cake meant
'fertility'. With relatively little leading of the informants, it was
possible to gain giggling assent to the suggestion that the cutting
of the first slice of the cake referred to the consummation of the
marriage. In such an interpretation, it was important that both
the bride and the cake were richly decorated in white. On this
occasion the cake had been home-made and sent away to be
professionally iced. It was *not* white, but decorated with peach-
coloured frills that matched not only the dresses of the brides-
maids (not the bride) but also the tablecloths, wall-hangings and
napkins of the reception. A local, symbolic resemblance had
been sacrificed to the demand for the general colour harmony of
a designer; any meaning had been sacrificed to a vacuous quest
for mere 'style'.

It was quite clear that the cutting of the cake marked the
transition to a more ribald stage of the reception, with many
allusions to future fruit of the marriage being bandied about.
This view of the sexual significance of the cake was bolstered by
the citing of the custom whereby the upper tier is kept for the
christening of the first child. Others remarked that couples would
have a similar cake for silver or ruby weddings, therefore the
cake 'looked forward' to these events and symbolized the perma-
nence of the relationship. Sociologically, the important thing
about the cake seems to be that everyone joins in the eating of it.
It is offered to all and consumed together like a sort of rich but
secular mass. Pieces will be sent to friends unable to attend the
reception.

Our imaginary ethnographer from the planet Mars would look
further. He would try to find out whether cakes were used to

mark events at other points of the English ritual cycle. He would soon discover what no informants volunteered, that English culture offers a series of festive cakes – Christmas cakes, birthday cakes – and their opposite, the minimal, undecorated pancake of Easter (opposed to festive cakes as poor is to rich, and associated with the self-denial of Lent). He might well identify the Christmas cake as Jesus's birthday cake, though no informant would admit to such an analysis. He would ask perhaps if there were cakes at funerals. 'No,' he would be told, 'no cakes, only cold meats.' The appropriateness of this last food would be only *too* clear. Informants might further add that champagne and group photographs would be shocking and out of place at a ritual of mourning and separation, a point we shall have to look at further.

Jim, my assistant in the field, dismissed out of hand any such elaborate attempts to incorporate the wedding cake into wider English patterns of the classification of events. He termed them 'fanciful'.

The problem of the wedding cake and its meaning is similar to the difficulties raised by many of the key symbols of English culture. A symbol is recognized quite generally as important, but acts as a sort of empty space that natives will fill with any meaning that is personally relevant to them. Such symbols seem to act to create a unity that papers over very real differences of viewpoint. Indeed, their only value may be to mark a commitment to Englishness.

Later Stages

After the speeches, the cutting of the cake and so on, the bride and groom change out of formal clothing, ready to 'go away'. This switches us to a new stage of the ritual. The couple are not ready to return to normal life. They move back towards normality but through another culturally specified state of betwixt and between: the holiday. Once again, they may expect the barrage of schoolboy humour and the sexual jokes of the stag night. The guests, too, are not returned to normality. For their benefit, the formal chairs and tables are cleared away and in their place is held an event of deliberate chaos – a discothèque.

Gifts

Gifts play a major part at weddings. Jim himself seemed a little baffled by the giving of presents. Gift-giving is an important part of most cultures, and in England it, like cakes, occurs on birthdays and at Christmas and weddings.

The English economy is a complex mixed/capitalist economy, the entrepreneurial ethic being heavily propagandized by government. Yet, whereas anthropologists stress the unity of culture, the natives never tire of doggedly dividing it into separate domains that they hold apart as having nothing to do with each other.

Some activities are determinedly kept out of the monetary sphere. One of the oddest aspects of English culture seen from Africa is the firm line drawn between money and sex/love. Any mixing, if not actually illegal, is certainly held to be morally degrading and the stuff of Sunday newspaper headlines. Hence modern English do not pay dowries or bride-prices, and regard cultures that do so as shocking. In the days of colonialism marriage payments were always suspected by the British of being a covert form of prostitution or slavery. The English family is regarded as a sphere within which the normal rules of economic interaction do not hold. The only circumstance in which the partners of a marriage calculate the economic value of their individual contribution is in the case of divorce. It is a sign that the lawyers have been called in and the marriage is effectively over.

For the moment, however, let us note the importance of gift-giving among the English. Gifts are separated from the monetary sphere by the insistence that any indication of their price be removed and that they should be regarded as mere material tokens of the real gift – the sentiment that lies behind them; hence aphorisms such as 'it's the thought that counts'. Cash gifts are the most difficult to make in such a culture and so a number of cultural forms have been devised to convert 'money' to 'gift' – book token, gift cheque and so on. Gifts should ideally be further removed from the economic sphere by lavish wrapping. (It is no contradiction of this that some shops provide a wrapping service for gifts – in return for payment.) The high point of this tendency is seen at Christmas, when richly wrapped gifts are presented as the fruit of an indoor tree.

The Smallwood wedding of Janet and Peter is relatively large, involving some 150 sit-down guests and many more at later stages of the evening. Weddings of this size are not unusual in the area.

At English weddings, friends and families from both sides offer gifts. A significant part of the ritual is that gifts should not be for individual partners but for the newly established household as a whole. The gifts are publicly displayed together with the names of the donors.

The same important distinction between gifts and commerce intrudes into the buying and selling of cattle. Philip Moss goes to Congleton market most weeks to sell cattle. But there is a curious custom there.

NB: Now, when you sold some cattle this morning, you went to the auction and I couldn't help noticing you held up a pound coin in your hand. What was that about? Was it a bribe for the auctioneer?
Philip: No. It wasn't a bribe. It's the old-fashioned luck penny and it's very noticeable in Cheshire. Everyone who sells cattle pretty nearly always gives the buyer a pound. Well, it's a very old-fashioned thing and it's called luck penny.

NB: What's the idea behind it?
Philip: I think the idea behind it is to show a little bit of
appreciation to the butcher who is buying the beast from
you and a little bit of encouragement for other butchers to
put in another bid . . . I think it's derived, you know, very
much from the old days of horse-selling.

True to an English perspective, Philip explains the luck penny in
terms both of a useful function and a bit of conjectural local
history. Yet the phenomenon is familiar from other parts of the
world. In the markets of West Africa, for example, if you buy a
certain amount of any merchandise – tobacco or whatever –
after it is measured out, the seller will add another measure as a
present. Muslims will explain that this is because their religion
warns of severe punishments for dishonesty but offers high
rewards for charity. Even non-Muslims do it, however, and
indeed a more general idea seems to lie at the base of it.

The luck penny might seem to be a welcome premium for the
butcher, who may be acting as the agent for someone else.
However, it is both expected and automatically allowed for in the
financial arrangements, like the West African market 'present'.
Philip rejected seeing it as a bribe. Its role is, indeed, much closer
to that of trading stamps. It takes part of the purchase price and
converts it into another category – that of 'present', 'free gift'. It
turns a commercial relationship into one of gift-giving.

Insiders and Outsiders

Invitations to weddings enter into exchange cycles.
Thus Janet, the bride, when asked why her wedding involved so
many guests, pointed out:

Janet: We've been to a lot of weddings. So you have to
invite your friends back.

The groom, too, was aware of this side of things:

Peter: Big weddings don't really do a big lot for me,
because hustle and bustle, you know, but on Janet's side it's
more of a ritual than getting married.
NB: What do you mean, a ritual?
Peter: Well, farmers tend to have big weddings and the
families get together and sort of like you've got to do it
really because people think of you having a big wedding.
NB: Whether you like it or not?
Peter: Whether you like it or not, yes.

Invitations to weddings also enter into the distinction between insider and outsider.

NB: How long have you been here, Bob [landlord of the
Blue Bell]?
Bob: Sixteen years now.
NB: Does that make you a villager or not?
Bob: I think just about now, yes. Actually, when I came here,
I was told it would take me years before I could get involved
in the village, but I think I was accepted quite quickly.
NB: Why was that do you think?
Bob: Well, I think I'd only been here a few months and
we got invited to a local farmer's wedding, so I thought,
'Well I must have arrived' because other people said, 'I've
lived here nine years and I don't get invited to these things.'

The distinction between insiders and outsiders is not simply one of the human community. It soon becomes clear that it extends to the animal population of the farm as well. I had always assumed that affection for animals is simply part of the town-dweller's view of the country, that breeding familiarizes contempt. In part this *is* true. Relations with animals at the market, not to mention the slaughterhouse, seem callous and unfeeling. They are regarded as mere commodities to be prodded, hit, killed. Yet a clear line is drawn between those beasts purchased simply for fattening and resale, and those that are a permanent part of the farm establishment. While all animals may have an identifying number, the dairy cows who become known as individuals to the farmer have a *name*. This is clear when Peter shows his breeding herd.

NB: You've given her [a pedigree cow] a name. Is that normal on a farm?
Peter: I do. That one there is always bumping people out of the way, so I call her Bunter, and this one never stops eating, so I call her the Pig, so I do call them names, yes, but it's not normal on a farm. I think dairy men tend to give cows names.
NB: But, I mean, is it going to bother you to sell these off one day?
Peter: Um, well, I don't think I shall ever sell these . . . maybe the calves, but I don't think I shall ever sell these. I've got too attached to them now.

Philip Moss makes the same distinction:

NB: Do you eat your own cattle?
Philip: Oh, we do. I don't think there are any farmers that wouldn't eat a piece of good prime beef off one of their own cattle. If it was a cow, which obviously you wouldn't have a piece of beef off, then I don't think you would want to eat Daisy or Megan, but in the case of a stall beast you don't get quite so attached to them.
NB: There's no sort of social relationship? They're not part of the family?
Philip: You haven't got the same . . . you know, obviously you like your cattle and you look after them and you become part of the scene with them, but you don't get quite the

same closeness as you would with a milking cow. A milking cow, you have a relationship with it fourteen times a week because you milk the thing and you've got to handle it, physically handle the cow, but not the same with a fattening animal. You know, you feed the thing and it's been fed *en bloc* with maybe eighty or ninety more so you don't get so attached to that animal as you do with a milking cow.

Continuity

Bob (landlord of the Blue Bell): It's a smashing village. The houses in this village that have changed since I've been here are always the same houses. The old families of the village . . . the farmers and farmers' families, they're the old village, you know. They're the people who can tell you things that went on in this village.

It is above all the relationship with the land that seems to constitute the ongoing unity of Smallwood. Informants are adamant that farms should not be divided.

Philip: Traditionally, you don't split farms.
NB: So, in a way, it's the people who belong to the farm, not the other way round.
Philip: That's right! That's right! It is.

To a town-dweller, the grip of Smallwood on its people seems extreme. The churchyard is full of the same surnames that one encounters nowadays around the village. The graves are carefully tended by descendants. Social life in Smallwood is rather like a low-budget movie, where the same characters keep turning up in all the minor roles.

Leonard Ford, for example, the organist at the wedding, also runs the family farm. Both sides of his family have been Smallwood people for six generations.

> *Leonard:* I've been organist now for fifteen years [he is 37 years old] and my grandfather was organist for forty and it was his wish that I should carry on the job. My grandfather on the Ford side, he was one of the top showing men, showing shorthorn cattle. We try to keep the showing side going. I'm on the church council. I'm on the parish council. I'm a trustee of the Furnival's charity. I'm representative of the parish council on the school governors . . .
> *NB:* How did you come by all those positions?
> *Leonard:* I suppose it's a bit like royalty, you're actually born to it. My great-grandfathers helped to carry the stone to build the church and the school and the vicarage many years ago. I went to the village school. I went to the local grammar school after that, went through Young Farmers, which all came to help with village life.

But is there no serpent in this Eden? Smallwood is a community where everyone's biography is public knowledge, where who you are and what you are are woven into the texture of your whole life. It certainly gives a clear sense of identity, but at what price? Doris Bracegirdle, teacher of generations of Smallwood children, sums it up:

> *Doris:* There's a tremendous sense of community and friendship and if anyone is in any sort of trouble or anything like that, the people are instantly on the phone, offering to help and that sort of thing. Probably, on the other hand, you will get this sense of people knowing – there's a magical grapevine in the village and everyone knows what's going on.

33

Endnote

Jim Batchelor, my Cockney informant, finds all this reminiscent of the old East End, much of which has now been replaced by soulless tower blocks. For him, as we have said, going back to the country is going back in time.

As an ethnographer, you are not expected to have personal reactions to events. As a native, you do. I have always found English weddings deeply depressing – not, I think, simply through male bias, where each wedding is seen as the capture of a free spirit by a social institution. Discussing it with Jim helped clarify the issue.

English culture, bolstered by our own folk psychology, pictures the individual as consisting, onion-like, of layers. Socialization is a mere veneer overlaying an emotional core – the *real* you. Other peoples, of course, have very different notions of such matters. In England the real is not for public display. It is a thing of the private world where emotional life occurs – at home behind the barriers we erect to keep the public world at bay. The West is often depicted as commercial and exploitative, yet, as we have already seen, such perspectives often exist in opposed pairs. The West is also the home of Hollywood love, endlessly promulgating saccharine-sweet images of affection and emotional fulfilment, of caring families and cherishing relationships. This, indeed, is the core protected by our notions of privacy, what we term our 'private life', and hedged round by rules of culture and the force of the law.

Public interventions, be they merely bureaucratic or religious *and* bureaucratic, have no place here. In a culture where emotions are the basis of marriage, weddings are a profound intrusion of the public into the private – what Jim would term 'a right liberty'. They claim to structure, regulate and express emotional life. All ritually evoked emotions have a ring of false-ness and hypocrisy. Given that emotional life is seen as personal and private – indeed spontaneous – ritual, public emotion is a contradiction in terms. Weddings are like the demonstrations of political ecstasy demanded by dictators. At the level of personal motivations, children go through such rituals to satisfy their parents, parents organize them as a duty to their offspring. Contemporary English culture is deeply suspicious of ritual.

2 Identity in the City

The brutal indifference, the unfeeling isolation of each in his private interest becomes the more repellent and offensive, the more these individuals are crowded together within a limited space and however much one may be aware that this isolation of the individual, this narrow self-seeking, is the fundamental principle of our society everywhere, it is nowhere so shamelessly barefaced, so self-conscious, as just here in the crowding of the great city.

> Friedrich Engels, *The Condition of the Working Class in England in 1844.*

IN SMALLWOOD a sense of identity is firmly communicated as part of public knowledge. It is ascribed rather than achieved. People are the way they are because of *who* they are. Insiders are seen as being mainly born into the community, growing up together and, ideally, marrying inside the group. In this, the local school is regarded as pivotal. It provides a loose system of age-grades that cross-cut all other divisions and a bedrock of biographical knowledge that can be built on to explain later life. The history of people's lives is thus very much in the public domain.

In the farming community an important part of identity lies in the land, which is seen as passing undivided from father to eldest son. Whether this in fact strongly structures what actually happens is another matter. (In the Middle Ages, after all, celibacy was also a virtue the popes passed also from father to son.) When Smallwood people speak of land, it is clearly seen as something that links generations together, being handed on 'like blood', and should not be sold except when in dire need.

In a wider context we have a name for such objects in which family identities are vested across the generations; they are known as heirlooms. Their power is enormous. At a national level, they operate through the institution of the monarchy. Yet perhaps the most immediate heirloom we all have is an insubstantial one – our father's (grandfather's, great ... grandfather's) surname, an endless fascination for those who want to find out their historical origins or establish for themselves an ethnic subculture. In the 'heads I win, tails you lose' world of sociological 'explanation', it is interesting to note that such a naming system has been seen either as the mark of a culture that lacks firm internal groupings (the name then acts as a compensation) or as the sign of a sexist culture characterized by obsessive grouping through males to the point of imposing it on language itself. From this we may infer the futility of a great deal of such 'explanation.'

The city operates by different principles from the country. Its

39

primary attractions are for the young and rootless, for whom it seems to encode the concept 'freedom' – from parental restraint, the limitations of past identities, the circumscribed possibilities of new contracts. Christine Restall works for McCann Erickson advertising and is an expert on modern British 'youth culture'. She was quite clear about the city's importance to the young.

NB: From what you've told us, it seems that no matter where young people in the UK live, in their heads they're living in the city. Is that correct?
Christine: We have to believe that's right at the moment. In the Seventies we were all into the misty countryside, but now it's all about urban decay as well, which is quite interesting. Maybe a reflection of the way young people feel about society and the age we're living in.

What then of the countryside? Christine was scathing:

Green wellies and trout streams and lady of the manor and all that kind of stuff? Yes, it's still a very powerful dream for an older generation. We've called the people who actually want to live that way, and indeed do, Lady Righteous in our woman study.
NB: What does Lady Righteous look like?
Christine: Her hair is fairly rigidly set in waves and she probably wears a twin set and pearls and a tweed skirt, and makes a lot of jam.
NB: She's a member of the Women's Institute?
Christine: Definitely yes and she really doesn't approve of women who go out to work outside the home. She's a little bit older than some of the other groups. She's actually married to the exact same male type, who we called Pontificator.
NB: What's he like?
Christine: Probably wears a wine-red cardigan.
NB: I have one at home.

We should note here how a single object is being used to typify a whole set of people with a predetermined set of opinions, tastes and values in a way that is immediately meaningful to members of our culture. How does this come about and what does it tell us about identity?

The Objectivization of Identity

... The gallery included a collection of objects designed according to 'False Principles'. It was known to one of its critics, writing in Dickens's *Household Words*, as a 'House full of Horrors', 'a gloomy chamber hung round with frightful objects ... curtains, carpets, clothes, lamps, and what not'. Cole himself believed that the object of this permanent exhibition was not to entertain but to instruct in the correct principles of taste. It was to be 'no lounge for idleness' but 'an impressive schoolroom for every one, including the general public'. The *Household Words* correspondent was 'ashamed of the pattern of my own trousers, for I saw a piece of them hung up there as a horror'.*

Man can be characterized as an obsessive creator of meaning systems. Some of these are conscious and even enshrined in the laws by which we define reality; others are unconscious. Some we defend as 'true', 'real' or, more lamely, 'useful'; others we use but may not be prepared to defend logically, in rather the way people in the UK seem to treat their horoscopes. Thus we expect to be able to tell a great deal about the internal states of people by their faces, their clothes, the way they talk. The fact that

* Asa Briggs, *Victorian Things*, London, Batsford, 1988.

experience is constantly denying our ability to make totally reliable predictions on the basis of such evidence does not discourage us from continuing to try to do so. Many of the discarded '–ologies' of the past are no more than the attempt to rationalize such folk expectations. Once they were science, now they are fantasy. Thus physiognomy – a passion of the late Victorian period – sought to relate facial features to character, while graphology saw the key as lying in handwriting and phrenology in the irregular topology of the cranium. Discarded systems are replaced by new ones to which new technologies give rise. Nowadays the first time we meet someone we have previously only spoken to on the telephone, we may well feel shock or surprise if they do not 'look like their voice'.

It is, curiously, in the Western cultures, where people make very few of the things they own, that we nevertheless expect to be able to draw inferences about owners from their possessions. We have even developed a profession that specializes in this and makes a good living at it. It is called the advertising industry. It, too, seeks to be a science.

The reasons why people buy particular things are recognized to be very complex. In former times, advertisers were very interested to collate behaviour according to socio-economic groups. The amount of detail about us as consumers is crushing.

Liz Watts is a bright, articulate woman in her early twenties, a planner with an advertising agency characterized as 'stylish' and 'high-profile'. Her job is to act as intermediary between client and 'creatives' (the people who think up the actual commercials), to make sure that each receives the proper information and that the commercial is correctly made to serve the client's purposes. I asked her to explain to me what sort of data about us she has to work with.

> *Liz:* [Information] comes in all shapes and sizes. Some of it
> is, say, from the government, so we have access to statistics
> that the government publish from a census and from other

surveys that the government conduct, which might be how
old the population is, how many of us there are, where we
live, how many people tend to live in one household . . . and
it can be as detailed as how much we spend on cheese a
week . . . how much the average shopping basket costs, those
sort of things we have access to. But obviously we have
other information which is in a way more useful, which is
of the more attitudinal kind, so that we can actually look at
what sort of people there are out there, not just how old
they are but how do they feel about life, how do they feel
about issues of the day, how do they feel about products . . .

Much endeavour is currently devoted to dividing the populace
into different 'life-style' groups. Thus agencies invent types – self-
explorers, experimentalists and so on – that purport to show
regularities in behaviour. These are unlike the data normally
used by anthropologists in that they are low-level statistical
glosses, trying to correlate, for example, political views and diet.
They are necessarily 'true' in that they merely seek statistical
regularities. On the other hand, other groupings within the same
data are always possible and the model has to be constantly
updated to remain in contact with the world it replicates. Especially important in modern marketing is the notion of 'badging'.

> *Liz:* 'Badging' really is wearing and buying products that
> very obviously say something about you because they are
> obviously a particular brand. So, for example, the newspaper
> you read is a very public statement about how you feel
> about the world, so the sort of person who might openly
> read the *Telegraph* is going to be quite a different person
> from the sort of person who likes to be seen reading the
> *Independent*, for example.

In other words, one can express an identity through exercising
choice in the things one buys. The notion of the brand is an

interesting one, seemingly an imposition on the world of objects of the notion of personality. It is, significantly, in the life of the city that identities are created and maintained in this way. In the fluid conditions of city life, with a gulf between work and private life and the anonymity of the street, a person can attempt to pass in as many identities as he can successfully perform.

Students of popular culture have tended to be dismissive of consumerism as merely a means of distracting the masses from the realities of economic exploitation. Fashion in objects is then simply an unimportant side-effect of over-production. Moreover, although people may claim that they are striving for individuality, they all end up looking more or less predictably the same. Individuality is therefore a sham. Only group identity remains. Yet perhaps we should see consumers less as passive cow-like creatures chewing on whatever is dumped in their mangers. The consumer can exercise choice in what he buys and so create identity. Indeed, most Westerners are no longer expert producers but have become expert consumers. This goes some small way to placing the relentless materialism of the West in a more positive perspective. We need material objects to confirm our social identity. In the West poverty is expressible not simply in terms of not having enough to eat, but also as being unable to sustain a proper identity through possessions.

Why, then, should correlations hold between the newspaper you buy and other areas of life? Why should people come in matching sets? Part of the answer is certainly that the correlations of advertising agencies are self-sustaining in their circularity. Many advertising campaigns that attempt to tie one product to others of high social standing are really advertising the 'identity through possessions' model of the world, a way of using objects that we assume to be univeral but is, in fact, only *one* way of using them. They tell us that if we drive a certain type of car, we *should* live in a particular sort of house and drink a particular sort of mineral water.

We discussed a number of television commercials with Denis

Lewis, art director of the same major advertising agency. He was quite clear that possessions are used in this signalling activity about self and are a major reason for selecting one brand as opposed to another. Indeed, it seemed as if there was no escape from meaning. When was a pair of shoes just something to put on your feet?

> *Denis:* I think all things say something about you. It might
> be 'I don't care' or it might be 'I think I'm wonderful – take
> a good look at me', but I think everyone finds their balance
> by buying the things that reflect them best.

The sorts of messages about self that Denis saw as being communicated by his advertisements for products he markets, such as K shoes, Pretty Polly tights and Levi's jeans, seemed to centre on notions of extreme individuality and self-command.

> *Denis:* It [a commercial for K shoes] is saying that you are
> a very confident, very self-assured and independent person
> really. I think you can buy a new image for yourself, but
> unless you actually feel at home with that image, I don't
> think it will work. You can only wear, at the end of the
> day, what you feel comfortable with.

At any one time concepts of identity may be assumed to focus on particular areas that take on a momentary prominence, only to disappear again from salience. (An example from recent years would be watches.) Clothes, on the other hand, are a long-running fixation. Since the Renaissance at least, trends in clothing have been a focus of concern for both men and women in the West. Principally, this elaboration of dress has occurred amongst the wealthy, the urban dwellers – in earlier times amongst the members of the court. The fulminations of the Church and the laws of the State alike tried to enforce a system whereby dress was a predictable and fixed mark of rank and profession, a reliable guide to one's place in the world. To wear inappropriate clothes was quite simply to lie about oneself.

In many parts of the world, this remains the case, though Western concepts are gaining ground as part of the cultural imperialism of our age. In the Third World clothes, coiffure and bodily decoration have traditionally been assigned to particular classes of people or ranked ages. They are not available to enter into the free play of concepts of identity as in our own culture. Such fixed systematic use of objects probably works only in cultures very different from our own. It should be remembered that in traditional societies until recently the world could be viewed as containing a finite number of objects without the constant invention of new possessions or the constant redesign of known ones. The introduction of new objects often involves a social revolution.

The concept of 'fashion' is a particularly Western idea, keyed in to the presupposition that material culture is in a constant state of flux and that novelty is to be regarded positively. Traditionally, fashion has centred on only two possibilities. The first is to be 'modern'; the second, to be 'out of date'. As we see from current advertisements, however, clothes are often seen as a statement about much broader issues. This is not entirely new. Dress has long had political overtones. The burning of bras and the wearing of trousers by women are inseparable in popular thought from feminism, just as concern with 'rational dress' characterized the early struggles of socialism. The theme was taken up at a recent Labour Party conference, which was, after all, divided by the issue of whether sharp suits, radio telephones and a Filofax were compatible with true socialism.

The innovation of mass-produced clothing has drawn the majority of the population into concern with dress at least to the point of exercising choice. But fashion now exists across all material culture. A bicycle, a fridge, a pen – all can become simply out of date or informative about oneself and certainly act as carriers of inbuilt cultural information. It is interesting that some few objects escape the cycle by which 'new' (good) becomes 'old-fashioned' (bad) becomes 'antique' (good again). These move directly from being 'new' to becoming 'classics' and therefore timeless (for example, the Volkswagen Beetle). A great deal of money would reward anyone able to discover what such objects have about them that confers this curious status.

There seems little reason why men and women should ride different bicycles, carry different umbrellas and bags; or why to have a tattoo is held to mark a man as violent or to wear an earring as effeminate. (Indeed, in recent years the connotations of a male earring have been largely reversed.) When objects pass from one culture to another, such cultural information as they carry may be lost or transformed. Thus nineteenth-century European travellers in Africa were surprised to find china chamber-pots used to serve food on the most discriminating tables. Such lines of demarcation as male/female are, however, important in our culture and tend to be imposed on all manner of objects. It is striking that English people will always defend such distinctions on grounds of utility. Thus, men need bigger umbrellas to keep their feet dry because they are higher from the ground.

The anthropological study of dress has classically tended to 'explain' its very existence in a number of ways:

1 People need to wear clothes to survive;
2 People wear clothes for modesty;
3 People wear clothes for purposes of display and to increase the sexual attractiveness of their bodies.

It is clear that even in our own climate point 1 holds for only part of the year and a few situations where control of the environment is impossible. Points 2 and 3 contradict each other but both may be true. They can be collapsed together by noting that the choice of clothes conveys messages about self and the nature of the event at which clothes are worn, as we saw at the Smallwood wedding. The absence of clothes marks the transition from public to private.

47

Public and Private – the Home

Although Liz Watts, our advertising planner, tends to see objects in terms of messages about identity, such a perspective is confined within firm limits. The problem of native informants and native ethnographers is that a world view is invisible when you are in it.

The building within which she works is extremely modern and spare. Pale greys and cool black metal surfaces, textured rubber tiles, small dramatic spotlights dominate the environment. I was told that on one occasion a whole consignment of pencils that had been ordered were thrown away because they did not *match* the building.

NB: Let's look about us a bit, in this building. If you had to judge this as an advertising prop, what message would you say that you were giving out about yourselves?
Liz: I think the message that comes out here actually is sort of hard work. The agency is actually designed to be like a factory. The idea of it is about creating an advertising factory, if you like, and all the décor or motif is quite subdued. I mean it's black and grey and white.
NB: But everything matches.
Liz: Everything matches.
NB: Do you sometimes feel that you have to match as well?
Liz: Fortunately not, no. I think the people are obviously what brings it to life and the background, the working environment, is very much there as a utilitarian thing to use, really. It's just a place to be or work and the thing that brings it to life are the people who work in it. It does all match, it does all fit together, but that's the way we work

too, we all fit together and do our separate jobs.

NB: Here you are, you see, an advertising person having told me how important these messages given out by objects are, yet your own working environment is totally practical and rational and sensible and not concerned with self-image.

Liz: Umm . . . There must be a fatal flaw in there somewhere! Yes, this also very stylish. I think the whole image of the agency, the way that it comes across, is very professional, is very stylish. As you say, everything fits together, everything looks as though it belongs here. I think that is quite important.

It so happened that Liz was moving house at the time we were making the film. It seemed too good an opportunity to miss. Liz and her husband were moving into a large Victorian terraced house in a rising area of London. It was the sort of place that an estate agent would describe as 'an excellent opportunity'. It offered the usual 'period features' (fireplaces, moulded ceilings and so on), but would clearly require a lot of work to convert it to the desirable residence of middle-class aspirations.

NB: So what's going to be your approach? Are you going in there with a totally new broom, total change, building work, the whole business?

Liz: No, perhaps not everything, but certainly quite a large proportion of it.

NB: So it's going to become a considered statement of your life-style, is it?

Liz: It is. It certainly is, yes.

NB: Do you sometimes wish you had thrown everything away and just moved in and started from scratch?

Liz: Oh no, no, because I think there's so much of you in your belongings. As I was saying to the removal guy, 'You've got my whole life in that van' because you collect things over the years and I think they matter to you. I don't think you can just

49

change overnight. I think you do always retain things. I mean,
I've got my teddy bear I had as a child in there somewhere.
NB: So your whole biography is tied up with those brown
cardboard boxes?
Liz: It is. It's frightening, isn't it, really? I mean, I wonder
what would happen if it all just disappeared overnight.
Would I be a different person in the morning?
NB: I wonder!

This is a quite different approach to possessions, one that sees
the link between a person and the objects he or she possesses as
reflecting not life-style or a matching, coherent, designer identity,
but biography. One is expected to be 'fond' of objects through
constant use and association. To throw them away because they
are old and should be replaced is to be unfeeling. As in the case
of the farmer's dairy herd or the members of the human family,
notions of cost-effectiveness are held to be inapplicable. These
things fall into a separate group to which one is affectively close.

Each item, moreover, is in some sense a material souvenir that
is evidence of the past. Objects are still approached through
notions of meaning, but the meaning is now not that of fashion
but more like that of the family photograph album. I suspect that
for many English people, their homes have this sort of meaning,
for where you live is the core of private identity. Home is where
your heart is, where you hang your hat, your castle.

The traumas of house-owning and -moving are legendary in
English popular culture. Mention of the subject swiftly produces
atrocity stories that others are eager to cap with their own tales
of even greater horror. We talked to Richard Landon, a professional removals man. He estimated that almost half the removals
with which he was involved were 'fraught'.

Richard: Women get fraught, especially if there's children
involved. I suppose it's difficult because you know they've
got to get to bed. We got permission to move in on one we

50

were doing in Morden last week at 11 o'clock at night and
that was only on account of the kindness of the people who
were moving out, because the contracts had been mucked
up, they couldn't trace solicitors and so forth and eventually
we managed to talk to them and say, 'Look, you've moved
into yours [your house], you must let these people move in.
They've got four kids and a cot.' They acquiesced and as
long as they didn't stay in the house, we could move the
goods in, as long as they went to a hotel. The exchange of
contracts and money changing hands is where most people
get frightened.

Yet, of all known peoples, the English are by far the most
insistent about actually buying and owning the houses they live
in. No hardship or inconvenience, it seems, is too great.

I recently had the experience of acting as host to some Indonesian hill tribesmen visiting England. They came from a
people long regarded as economically 'irrational' in that they
sink much of their wealth in buffalo that are then slaughtered in
large numbers at their funerals. They, however, found the English staggeringly irrational in the amount of money, proportion
of income and amount of effort that they devote to owning their
own home. Why, they asked, should anyone spend so much on
owning a home he could never be in because he had to go out to
work to pay for it? The answer is that English personal identities
are very much tied up with the home whereas these Indonesians
were more concerned with the glorious ancestral houses that
their ancestors derived from rather than the modest houses that
they themselves lived in.

It is not mere legal and practical problems that arise in
moving house. Liz was eloquent on the embarrassment of looking
at other people's houses in their presence.

Liz: You have to be quite polite really and not show your
shock at some horrible wallpaper or furnishings that you

might not like, so I think it is quite difficult, but, then, on the other hand, everyone is on the other end of it too, so I think that everyone understands that. I always try to go round with as blank a face as possible actually, so that they are not feeling I am criticizing their décor.

NB: But when you're on the receiving end, you feel pretty much that you're being judged and that your whole character is on display, you as a person?

Liz: Yes, quite definitely. You *do* feel quite territorial about it . . . The fact that someone might not like your colour scheme or your wallpaper, I mean, it is quite hard to take really. Someone criticizing your taste, isn't it? And if people show their feeling on their face by grimacing at something *you've* got, it does hurt really.

What is happening is that our most private possession, that which tells most about our inner self, is being put on public display and – even worse – evaluated in cash terms.

We spoke to Patrick Meller, an estate agent, about it. Patrick is young (25), ambitious, clearly upwardly mobile. He manages a branch of a large chain of estate agents in Hayes. Hayes is basically a 1930s 'quality' suburb, complete with traditional high street and railway station for the large number of commuters. The other mark of its quality is the existence of trees on the streets. It is an area of houses, semis or detached, rather than flats, each with a small garden fore and aft. It has a predominantly white population and is a place mainly for young married couples, where most domestic activity happens behind regularly repainted front doors – definitely 'not a place for street life'. Schools are important, as is the existence of the green belt. Indeed, the local residents' group, the Hayes Village Association, insists that the 'real' Hayes still *is* a village and devotes much time to the planting of trees.

Patrick is aware that his own position as middleman makes him open to hostility.

Patrick: Moving is a very stressful time for anyone and I
think for the majority of people it probably brings out the
worst side of the nature, which is understandable because
they are moving the whole centre of their life really. You
can be the target for someone's hostilities when you're not
necessarily to blame.
NB: It's unfortunate, isn't it, in that it's sort of built in.
You're putting a price on the house, the focus of identity,
the family. In some sense it's as if you were a pimp coming
round, putting a price on the virgin daughter.
Patrick: That's right.

This is the core, then, of the estate agent's job, the expression
in monetary terms of the family home, the intrusion of the
commercial sphere into the very heart of the private.

The striking thing about Hayes is that although large numbers
of houses were put up at the same time and began as identical
products, they now show an incredible variety.

Patrick: Every house is different. When you go into a
property, they're all decorated – different ideas. There's
everyone's stamp, their personality is stamped on their
property.

The English house is a highly structured affair. In Hayes it
begins with the front garden. Patrick is very firm that the Hayes
front garden is important. It must be kept in good order – like
the carefully scrubbed front steps of gardenless, terraced houses
– but it is unthinkable that anyone would ever sit in it. Such a
thing could happen only in the *back* garden. The front is the face
of the house.

The next most important barrier is, of course, the front door,
with all its various locks and signalling devices. The front door is
again a focus of elaboration. Gimcrack, boxy houses often sport
an expensive 'Georgian' door with brass 'door furniture'. Under

English law it is a particularly serious offence to force entry to a private home. Interestingly, English people whose homes have been broken into often speak of the experience in terms of violation and rape. The home is clearly a powerful symbol of the integrity of the individual.

Immediately behind the door, off the hall, are the various public rooms. In former times, many English homes had a 'front room' that would be kept for 'best' and receiving visitors, and was not to be used by members of the family. It too was part of the public face of the house. This custom has now fallen largely into disuse. The rooms are segregated according to the physical functions performed in them, sitting, eating, defecation and so on, again stressing that the house is an acutely *physical* object and modelled on the human body. Ideally, functions should not be mixed. Thus, to serve dinner in the bedroom can be justified only on grounds of infirmity. Most strongly segregated are rooms for washing and excretion, simultaneously the most public (in that all have access to them) and the most private (in that they are obsessionally locked). Rooms are variously accessible to out-siders. Access to the sitting-room alone implies formality, to the kitchen less so. Bathrooms may be used with permission.

Most important are the bedrooms. These, where the most private sexual functions are exercised, are held to be the most personal rooms and access to them is always regulated, except in the case of very young children. Access to such 'sexual' parts of the house is controlled as access to sexual parts of the body. Domestic animals will often be prohibited in these areas. One knocks on another's bedroom door as on a front door. The modern English ideal is for each individual or sexual couple to have their own bedroom and for new unions to require a new house, so that the distribution of bedrooms supplies a map of sexual identities. Not surprisingly, it is these areas of a house that are most firmly stamped with the character of the owner. Adults normally do this through choice of furnishings, teenagers through putting up pictures of sporting interests and muted sexual fantasies – in a very real sense they spread their images all over the walls.

When visiting houses for appraisal, Patrick was never in any doubt which members of a family owned a particular bedroom or what was their age and sex. Bedrooms of heads of households and sitting-rooms were almost always in the same styles, reflecting the dominance of house heads or their wives on the house generally. The English house is a fascinating cultural document and reading its meanings brings all the forbidden titillation of steaming open other people's mail.

A curious English fixation is with the hearth. Although open fires are largely redundant for purposes of practical heating, they are still of great importance to the sitting-room. Enormous sums may be spent on ornate fireplaces, which are even removed from one house to be attached in another. There have been recent cases of thieves stealing fireplaces from unoccupied houses. In addition, various sorts of imitation fires, of great cost and elaboration, have been devised. These may well be bought and installed although they make no useful contribution to heating.

English houses are based upon the presupposition of a fireplace, which governs the orientation of furniture, at least in the sitting-room, where sitting positions focus upon it. One of the striking curiosities of British colonial rule was the insistence of expatriates on constructing fireplaces even in the hottest tropical climate. This was clearly an important cultural need. English rooms are often found awkward by those from other cultures, as people engaged in informal conversation do not face each other directly but may well be staring into an empty grate. In modern English rooms a rival for attention is, of course, the television set. Such clashes of prominence are frequently settled by standing the television beside the fireplace.

How may one investigate this curious clinging to redundant technology? The English justify their retention of fireplaces in terms such as 'cosiness'. It is often explained that such fires are used only on special occasions: Christmas, when friends come round for dinner, occasions of hospitality. It is somehow felt that they make a room more welcoming – the equivalent of candles on a dinner table. Explorations of the native concept of 'cosiness' suggest that at the heart of the term is a sense of the distinction between inside and outside. It is no contradiction of this that one informant remarked, 'Open fires always make me think of the camp fire at Scouts. You're in that little circle of heat and light with all your friends and nothing outside it exists. You're really together.' Outside may be cold and threatening; inside is warm and safe. The fireplace is, then, more than a heating apparatus. It is a recognizable cultural device for stressing the boundaries of the house, its importance as a sanctuary and the worth of hospitality – almost a shrine of household values and the counterpart of that other great possession, the front door.

Sense of Self

In Hayes, we were lucky enough to join in a 'perfume party'. These events are organized in a home environment, that is, in a context that seeks to duck associations of commercialism and to sell cheaper 'interpretations' of well-known fragrances to housewives through personal contacts. After a short introduction by a demonstrator, participants are encouraged to try perfumes that suit their personalities. To maintain a coherent persona, it seems, you have to blast out your identity on this channel too.

This marketing of smells is the application of 'personality through possessions' to the most evanescent of the senses. It has been argued that smells are especially able to evoke memories and associations in that they lie largely outside the organizing power of language. Western words for smells are notoriously imprecise and underdeveloped, and our use of them – especially outside the Roman Catholic Church – comparatively unorganized. Here, they are identified by numbers. Colette Gibbons, the demonstrator, explained how such choices were made. There were, of course, certain smells considered appropriate to little old ladies, such as lavender, but Colette regarded perfumes as, above all, markers of mood.

> *Colette:* If I was feeling rather poorly, I'd have a little
> light, fresh, fruity one. If I felt very dynamic and extrovert –
> I'd had a good day – I'd have a much stronger oriental
> spicy one or maybe the musk.

But there is a distinction between male and female. Female perfumes contain:

> *Colette:* Rose, Tudor rose, delphinium, geranium, lavender,
> and in the men's there's always the leaves, the barks, the
> resins, cedarwood, sandalwood, mosses, lichens.

Nowadays, however, women may wear 'male' perfumes as part of the opening up to women of new roles. Women maintained that they even had a working perfume, which they would wear while doing the chores. Special events, parties, dinners and so on were marked by a more expensive scent. It seems that you're never fully dressed without a smell.

Endnote

We returned with Jim Batchelor, my native inform-ant, to the East End to try to compare it with the memories he had of it as a friendly place.

NB: So this is the East End, Jim. This is your old stamping

ground, what you dreamed about when you were in the
country.

Jim: Well, it's not quite as how it used to be, is it?

NB: If you'll excuse my saying so, it looks a bit bleak.

Jim: It used to be nice. It used to be like a little village on
its own once. You used to have little cottages round here.
Everybody used to know everybody else. But since these
high-rises have been here it's just sort of knackered it. It's
nothing at all now.

It was true. There seemed little but a brooding mix of grey tower
blocks looming over the newer Docklands development of Toy-
town architecture crammed with possessions, new identities for
old. Even for Jim, a confirmed town-dweller, the sort of community he remembers is no longer here but in the country.

3 Bodies of Knowledge

In hospital, I had a sort of revelation. I was ill in New York. I was wondering where I had previously seen young ladies who walked like my nurses. I had time to think about it. I finally realized it was at the pictures. When I got back to France, I noticed how common was this way of walking, especially in Paris; the young ladies in question were French and they, too, walked in the same way. In fact, thanks to the cinema, the American walking fashions had begun to appear in France. This was an idea that could be generalized.

Marcel Mauss, *Sociologie et Anthropologie.*

A S THE QUOTATION from Mauss suggests, there is no such thing as the natural body. Human bodies are inevitably cultural products. The most basic, physical activities – walking, eating, defecation – are already heavily marked by culture. The rhythmic strut of West Indian males and the mincing tread of Thais are equally learned behaviour and subject to interpretation and misinterpretation. The gait of American ladies was as much a problem in London as in Paris. When American ladies first appeared in large numbers on the streets of the Edwardian capital, they were appalled to discover that, because of their characteristic gait, they were generally taken for prostitutes and approached accordingly. In other parts of the world quite distinct realities hold for such imagined universals as the need for sleep, sex and bowel evacuation.

Yet, to the man in the street, the physical body would seem to be about as close as we could come to a universal in the study of human affairs. There are, to be sure, minor variations between the inhabitants of the various parts of the globe, dissimilarities of hair texture and its distribution, skin colour and stature. It is uniquely human to have taken such differences and built them into a theory of evolutionary stages, moral standing and political power such as has been constructed by the West over the past few centuries of interaction. For the body is not just a vehicle that a mental ego inhabits, it is a medium of thought and expression that enters into our most basic concerns.

The Dirty Body

A good place to see our notions of the body writ large is in a strip club. These establishments rest on some very basic cultural notions about the human body. For us, the normal body is clothed. An essential part of the imaginary 'Naked Ape' is its insistence on using clothing to create a cultural world. It is extraordinary that to completely remove one's clothing in public is a criminal offence. The English on the one hand find it absurd that Arab women may hide their faces in public, and on the other are shocked by African males leaving their genitals uncovered. Paradoxically, both deviations from English usage, 'excessive' and 'insufficient' use of clothes, are equally regarded as proofs of primitiveness. Yet the English operate a similar distinction between public and private parts of the body, the only difference lying in those parts that are regarded as actually one or the other. The classification is the same – the borders have been shifted.

The strip club deliberately flouts normal English rules in return for money. It shows 'private parts' as a public spectacle. People pay money to just *look*. Jim Batchelor and I had rather different views of the matter.

> *Jim:* It's worth the money though, innit? Don't you think?
> *NB:* Well, I once tried explaining it to an African
> schoolteacher and he just couldn't grasp it. I mean, it was,
> he said, like spreading out a good meal and then taking it
> away before you could eat.
> *Jim:* Well, he's a slow eater, isn't he?

Such a display sets itself up in violation of at least two major dividing lines of English culture: public/private and sexual/commercial. In doing so, it exploits two major alibis: 'art' and the 'naturalness' of the human body. To this, Jim was able to add a third, health:

> *NB:* You don't think this has anything to do with some
> deep, male chauvinist bias of our culture, a capitalist
> tendency that sees human flesh as a commodity to be bought
> and sold?
> *Jim:* No. It's just clean fun, isn't it? It helps people out.

You get blokes that have never seen a woman's body before and they come to these places to see it. It's harmless fun.
NB: It's good for you?
Jim: Oh yes, very good for you.
NB: So that's why you're here, because it's healthy?
Jim: Yes. It takes a lot off your mind.

It is not surprising to find such places hedged round with moral censure and rules that seek to limit their sphere of operations. Some people would see such performances as 'dirty' or at least as an area characterized by a great deal of hypocrisy. Thus in English newsagents it is all right to sell pornographic magazines as long as they are kept on the top shelf. Yet culture is a thing of many layers. We are here at the level of 'rules about rule-breaking'.

The Pure Body

When I was a child, the physical was held to be rather a disgrace. Men especially were expected to take no obvious pains over their appearance. To do so was to give rise to suggestions of the most outrageous moral degeneracy. Sport was encouraged as a means of learning 'team spirit', how to triumph without gloating and how to lose without bursting into tears. It was also a way to control the unruly flesh and its temptations.

Nowadays this is quite reversed. Physical activity and dieting are encouraged as a means of enhancing health and sexual attractiveness. Monastic self-discipline is now the road to a deeper self-indulgence. Fast today, to feast tomorrow. Sport, moreover, becomes a justification for wearing the physically revealing sportswear that has been the focus of creative fashion for some years and is now the everyday dress of many.

In a world of negotiable identities one's own physical appearance is something a person may well be held responsible for. Current concern with gymnasia, plastic surgery and body building is simply part of the notion of mirror identity. You are what the reactions of others tell you you are.

We visited a health farm, located in the plush Surrey countryside of the paunched stockbroker belt. The building was that of the country retreat of an industrial baron, a façade that spoke of commercial success and the affluence of Home Counties squirearchy. According to the management, it was patronized by all sorts of people. However, those on display were principally the wealthy of jowly middle age. I asked Jane Roberts, an eminently healthy-looking consultant, why people came to the clinic.

> *Jane:* A lot of people still feel that they've come here just
> to diet, but I don't think that actually happens any more.
> About 20 per cent of the people only come to actually go on
> a diet. The rest of the people come here because they're tired
> and they don't want to go off on holiday somewhere, so
> they come here to unwind, because they're very stressed
> and they've been working very hard.
> *NB:* So this is a sort of retreat from the outside world?
> *Jane:* Yes, it is. They drive through the gates and they feel
> that they're coming to a place where they're going to be
> cosseted and looked after and they can shut the outside
> world away from them.

This is also a familiar model of the world. Health is regarded as natural. Illness is a departure from that state, which can be viewed either as a punishment for evil or caused directly by the 'unnatural' way we live, a product of culture. If we lived naturally, all would be well, but, instead, we sin against the world. Concepts of naturalness are usually a stick used to beat someone into line. Here they are used to question a whole way of life, as we saw in the myth of the country. Diseases have long been regarded as the fruit of self-indulgence: smoking leads to cancer, drinking to cirrhosis (formerly the emphasis was on gout), sexual licence to AIDS (formerly the emphasis was on VD, and before that, leprosy). Indeed, diseases have appeared and disappeared almost on demand. Hysteria was a nineteenth-century affliction of women held to be under-used in childbearing, while the alleged terrible medical effects of male masturbation were much written about in an age of unmarried younger sons. Early in this century agoraphobia assailed women compelled to leave the house, which they had considered their proper sphere of activity. Currently, anorexia is said to attack those (especially women) who seek to control their lives through their bodies – a disease of inadequate consumption.

The activities of the health farm, diet, exercise, massage, aromatherapy, seem to be divisible in two. Some aim to discipline the recalcitrant flesh. Here suffering is quite important. Your suffering is the measure of how much 'good' you have done yourself. This comes through in the language of the instructresses. 'This is not a holiday!' they shout. 'Work! Imagine you're hitting me! Hate your instructress!'

People here are giving up control over their bodies in a way they have not done since childhood. In our culture, coming into power over your own body is the mark of full, mature membership of the community. Many men remember growing hair long enough to touch the shirt collar when they were at school as a major victory over the whole of society. Sexuality enters into it too. Thus we define childhood as an asexual state and hold children to that with laws that deny them the right to make sexual decisions about themselves. We have recently started removing the sexuality of the mentally deficient. There is evidence that the cessation of sexual activity is crucially involved in our definition of people as 'old'.

Other dominant images of the health farm are those of cleansing, washing, steaming, evacuating – reflecting how much of the evil of culture you have got out of yourself. The environment of the clinic reflects this cleanliness just as that of the strip club was greasy and besmirched.

Other activities centre on pampering the flesh through cosmetic cosseting: facials, massage, waxing and so on. The clinic has its own hairdresser and boutique, and provides a reassuring justification for assimilating health to attractiveness.

> *Jane:* I think if you look better, you automatically feel better. If you've actually been eating sensibly and keeping yourself looking good, you automatically feel better.
> *NB:* So a lot of looking after your body happens inside your head?
> *Jane:* Yes. I think it is terribly important that these two are linked together.

For me, the massage was the message. First, not just any oil was used. Aromatic oils are employed variously to stimulate or relax by their smell. Massage inevitably makes you aware of your body by the mere fact that it exposes much of it to dispassionate gaze and it is then outlined by the touch through the offices of the masseur. The suffering aspect of it becomes clear only the next day.

I once had a massage in an Indonesian village, which was splendid. The man was very annoyed at how sloppily Europeans were put together and he massaged for about an hour, and for a whole day everything worked. Then, of course, the next day I couldn't even walk.

Diet is a great concern of the clinic. I spoke to Jillian Adams, a dietician. Our relative situations were immediately apparent from our dress, myself having been coaxed into a track suit to signify sporting endeavour, she in a nurse's uniform of formidably starched crispness.

> *Jillian:* I think one of the most important messages that I

am trying to get across here is getting in touch with the body. Even if they're here for two or three days, what they're doing is getting food for the right reasons. They're not eating habitually. They're not eating . . . to calm down.

Even so, Jillian wryly confesses that most residents find the menu posted on the notice board the day's most compulsive reading.

Eating, like dress, is one of the traditional ways of establishing who you are. You are what you eat. So if you eat healthily and dress healthily, you *are* healthy. Healthy food is 'high in fibre, low in fat, low in salt, low in sugar and, of course, no alcohol'. It involves a lot of raw vegetables and has a decidedly monastic feel. It is, inevitably, 'natural', but some boundaries are too firm to be crossed: there is no raw, bloody flesh served here.

Control of the boundaries of your body is a very powerful way of defining yourself – as many of the world's religions have shown – so the transformation effected by health farms may be expected to be largely a matter of redefining yourself in new terms.

It was interesting to see an institution devoted to the undermining of the Cartesian mind–body duality that philosophers and anthropologists never tire of rubbishing. There is a real sense in which a health farm reduces you to your body as the strip club does the stripper. Whereas most of the time you are unaware of your fleshy envelope, here you are made aware that you have a body twenty-fours hours a day.

I suspect that Jim was more in tune with mainstream views on the subject than the staff's clinic. His model of the human body is the car, a mere machine.

NB: The only question is, Jim, whether *your* body is quite a Porsche or whether it's more of an old banger.
Jim: Well, it's a Ford Cortina really, just carries on and on!

Beneath the joke lies a serious point, for it is the image of the body as a machine that underlies much of Western medicine, and many things follow from it. Faults can be diagnosed mechanically and functionally; a firm line can be drawn between physical and mental illnesses; a clear line divides health and sickness, medical and social problems; defects can be solved by substituting new spare parts. It is also a model of restricted optimism. The car you have is severely limited in its development potential. After running-in, it is all downhill. Wearing out is natural and inevitable.

Interestingly, our culture already has the cautionary myths of 'the body a machine' in Frankenstein and the uncontrollable robot beloved of science fiction.

The Medical Body

The medical men have an imposing temple, or *latipso*, in every community of any size. The more elaborate ceremonies required to treat very sick patients can only be performed at this temple. These ceremonies involve not only the thaumaturge but a permanent group of vestal maidens who move sedately about the temple chambers in distinctive costume and headdress . . .

The supplicant entering the temple is first stripped of his or her clothes. In everyday life the Nacirema avoids exposure of his body or its natural functions. Bathing and excretory functions are performed only in the secrecy of the household shrines . . . Psychological shock results from the fact that bodily secrecy is suddenly lost upon entry into the *latipso*. A man whose wife has never seen him in an

> excretory act suddenly finds himself naked and
> assisted by a vestal maiden while he performs his
> natural functions into a sacred vessel . . . Female
> clients, on the other hand, find that their naked
> bodies are subjected to the scrutiny, manipulation
> and prodding of the medicine men.*

The medical body is charted by maps quite different from the other bodies with which we are acquainted. Its language is largely Latin (or Latin-derived). It dispassionately charts the sexual areas but is doggedly unerotic. Should one translate the anatomical references of an erotic novel into medical terms, they cease to be pornographic and become merely comic. Firm rules decree that, to the medical practitioner, all bodies are equally uninteresting sexually and aesthetically. To deny such a rule is to risk being struck off for 'unprofessional conduct'.

Yet, while it aims at the universality and moral neutrality that are the ideals of the natural sciences, medicine is unremittingly a very *social* science. Its boundaries are not immediately given but are clearly culturally defined. Things move in and out of the medical domain. Thus in 1974 the American Psychiatric Association decided *by vote* that homosexuality was not an illness and overnight it ceased to be one. The status of mental disorders and criminality as illnesses are similarly subject to change, depending not primarily on their own qualities, but on changing views on such general topics as personal responsibility, innate tendencies and social determination – in fact, anything that can affect our view of the individual. Alcoholism and addiction generally have a similarly awkward and variable relationship with the medical and legal professions. Even the notion of death, with its focus on loss of individual consciousness, is cultural rather than physical. As a rule of thumb, it is the case

* Horace Miner, 'Body Ritual among the Nacirema [American backwards!]', *American Anthropologist*, 58, 1956, 503–7.

that 'medicalization' of a problem, the declaration that it is an illness, removes the sense of individual responsibility.

In English culture health is regarded as the norm from which illness departs. In many parts of the world one's illnesses may be attributed to the malice of others through the mechanism of witchcraft. English metaphysics do not permit of such a possibility. For many English people, such as Jim, the incidence of illness is regarded as random bad luck. It lies *beyond* explanation. If you are a 'lucky' person, you do not get ill. If you are 'unlucky', you do.

We went to Dorchester, Dorset, to see medicine in action. We were lucky enough to find two very different doctors who let us observe something of the way they live and talked to us about their views on contemporary medicine. The first was Dr Charles Campion-Smith, a general practitioner in his forties. Charles works in a group practice with two other doctors and a trainee. He is married to Sue, formerly a midwife, and they have three young children. He very much rejects the notion that doctors are there just to treat diseases, an approach that he still finds in his trainees.

> *Charles:* Some people would say the first few months is spent 'untraining' them, trying to take them out of rigid ways of thinking and be system-based. We see diseases *in people*, then get them to move away from that and see families who may be sick and not functioning in some way that does not actually fit into a hospital-based category.

Consequently, for Charles, it is not just the line between mind and body that has to go: 'Mind, body, family. We don't stop at our skin.' Yet this can bring difficulties.

> *Charles:* The worry is if you respond to that and turn life's problems into disease. A person who is unhappy after a bereavement or after the death of a spouse, if you give them

tablets, for instance, you actually deny that being unhappy after a loss is a normal thing and make it into an illness.
NB: What do you do if people come to you suffering from depression? They're unemployed, they've got bad housing, life is really not very good for them. Do you just say to them, 'Well you're right to be depressed. Your life is deeply depressing,' or do you find yourself being required by the patient, as a doctor, to give them a prescription?
Charles: That's one of the biggest dilemmas, I think. What one has to do is try to separate the people who are appropriately unhappy and the people who actually have depression as an illness, which is even more than deep unhappiness . . . More often, people are just helped by understanding and sympathy.

His wife, Sue, has observed the same medicalization of child-birth.

Sue: There are many more male obstetricians than there are female and it can be that it [childbirth] is treated like an illness. I mean, things can go wrong, but I would feel it's a natural process.

Of course, what is 'natural', as we would expect, also varies enormously from culture to culture, just as do judgements about 'appropriate unhappiness'. Consider, also, many of the effects of ageing. In the past these have been regarded as inevitable, yet the discovery of 'slow viruses' and cumulative environmental toxins now lead them to be regarded more as diseases. We might now see a parallel with an old Egyptian medical problem. In parts of Egypt the waterborne disease bilharzia is endemic in the male population who work in irrigation ditches. The first symptoms, intestinal bleeding, occur in boys about the same time as menstruation appears in girls and it has been difficult to change the view that these are totally natural counterparts of each other. As girls grow up, they menstruate; as boys grow up, they bleed intestinally. Both are seen, in that culture, as 'natural'.

The point is that, increasingly, it is to doctors that the English turn for statements of what is natural and normal. The priest has been largely displaced as a source of guidance, even in moral matters or just as a source of comfort. The doctor, as our local representative of scientific knowledge, is nowadays the professional whose specialist training is a means of gaining ritual definitions.

NB: Sickness is a state that the doctor can either withhold or grant?
Charles: Yes, and lots of people come to us quite willing to accept that we may not know what is wrong with them, but as long as we can tell them what's *not* wrong with them, that's sufficient. Another thing we ask is why they came. 'Did you come for medicine to make it better or is it a question of knowing what it is?' And a lot of them say, 'Oh, as long as I know what it is, I'm quite happy to put up with the symptoms,' and we've not actually put it into the 'normal' but we've put it into the 'not significant' group.

Charles seems to have a rather different notion of responsibility for health from Jim, one closer to the health-farm ethic.

NB: One of the things at the health farm, they did seem to have a notion of health as a positive thing. You were responsible for your health as an individual. You bore the burden on yourself. It was a duty to be healthy.
Charles: Yes, I think we have a responsibility for illness. If it's all someone else's problem, I can just hand it over, but actually you have a responsibility for yourself and there are things you can do to help yourself get better . . . We are increasingly saying we're not giving answers, we're giving information.

72

As a non-smoking vegetarian and habitual cyclist, Charles puts these principles into operation. Yet, strikingly, the power of the doctor is not so lightly removed. In the scenes we filmed in Charles's surgery the patients were very clearly receiving instructions rather than advice and preferred it that way. Authoritarian habits die hard too. A patient touching a skin infection was told snappily, 'Get your fingers out! Leave it alone!' – an instinctive distinction between the healing touch of the physician and the interfering digit of the patient.

Charles's approach to medicine, then, was one that was not restricted to the treatment of disease. He saw himself as giving advice about a whole life-style, of which disease was only one aspect. This is a fairly new approach to illness in the 'scientific' West. To anyone who has worked *outside* the West, it has a decidedly familiar ring. In Africa a man will say to you, 'My cow's fallen down the well, my wife's run away with the blacksmith and now I've got this rash on my arm' and to him they're all part of the same thing.

Our other doctor was strikingly different from Charles. Patrick Jeffrey is a general surgeon specializing in diseases of the bowel. He has been a consultant for eight years and spends most of his time in the Dorchester and Weymouth hospitals, but also sees out-patients in Bridport and Lyme Regis. Not surprisingly, he fits pretty closely his own idea of what a surgeon should be.

Patrick: First of all, you've got to like what you're doing.
I think you've got to be the sort of chap, actually you'd be a
sort of all-rounder, a chap who likes people, likes talking,
likes doing things with his hands, is prepared to work hard
and who has an ability to get on with people . . . I always
used to say a good doctor is someone who can get on with
chaps in the pub, the church, the village store and at the
local squire's cocktail party. If you can get on with all of
that mix, you're going to be all right. If you can talk your
way through that lot, then you can talk your way through
out-patients and around the wards and everywhere.

73

These are not merely patrician social and verbal skills. They are an essential part of the healing process.

> *Patrick:* You have got to instil confidence, so I think you
> have to be a bit of an actor. Everyone I know who is a
> surgeon is a basic extrovert.

But what of the skills of surgery as opposed to general practice?

> *NB:* In the medical world you're more what? . . . the S A S
> end of the market, aren't you? You're the intervention squad.
> *Patrick:* Yes. I've just finished reading a book which had
> a very good phrase and I think it was 'the hostage rescue'.
> You can definitely pick out the people who are going to be
> surgeons. Very occasionally . . . there are physicians who
> have the surgeon's mentality, but you very often find those
> are the sort of physicians who like doing things actively and
> they intervene with various instruments.
> *NB:* So a surgeon is more of a solver than a carer?
> *Patrick:* The surgeon is a *doer*!

Patrick went on to stress the need to be able to take decisions quickly, to take responsibility, to head a team and to have self-confidence. These remarks were made while he was being filmed carrying out a mastectomy. It sounded very much like a description I was given later, when we were looking at the Territorial Army, of a good military leader. The comparison is not gratuitous. One view of medicine treats it as a war against illness. Thus informants will speak of 'the war against cancer', 'battling against disease', 'fighting for life'. This view is confrontational and uses the gleaming machines of modern technology to kill and destroy pathogens and growths. On the other hand, the military use many images derived from medicine, and 'surgical' is nowadays the highest word of praise for a military 'operation'.

Rationality and Ritual

To enter an operating theatre requires special permission. It is the high temple of science, and therefore is also a ritual space with its boundaries firmly controlled. A doctor has a privileged relationship with our bodies. He is licensed to see us naked. Modesty is out of place. 'It's all right,' he will say while probing our most intimate orifices and personal secrets, 'I am a doctor.' There is a need to ritually mark off this status and place. Charles Campion-Smith remarked upon it.

> *Charles:* Somebody I know quite well because of children at school came in and the first bit of interchange was as friends – 'How are the kids?' – and then I say, 'Right, sit down', and he said, 'You changed gear and became somebody different.' You stop being the friend meeting at school . . . move it from chit-chat, which more medically is metaphorically putting on my white coat, and things come out then which, I think, would not be possible to talk about had I still been the friend.

What of the surgeon? Surely what he does is governed by the needs of scientific hygiene? We have all seen on television the draconian measures taken by surgeons.

> *NB:* Can you tell us what you're doing?
> *Charles:* I'm going to wash.
> *NB:* Three times, is that right?
> *Charles:* Well, the idea is to wash so that you get rid of all the bacteria on your hands, so there used to be a tradition of standing there for ten minutes and rubbing away with the scrubbing brush . . . The bacteriologists have shown us that all that does is produce the bacteria coming from the depths of the skin and does actually no good at all . . .

So much of what we 'know' about the hygienic precautions taken by surgeons no longer applies. Most of them are not necessary, yet we continue to feel they *ought* to be necessary, like that totally pointless dab of alcohol on the arm before an injection. In fact, to a layman, the preliminaries of surgery seem offensively undramatic.

NB: You don't have to go and have a total shower or shave off your eyebrows or anything like that?
Patrick: No. There used to be a system in days gone by of changing all your clothes and people used to come in with just greens on, as we've got now, but with no underpants, no socks, but most people have now given that up. It goes to show that it didn't do much good.

What then of the mask? At least they still insist on that.

Patrick: You and I are wearing masks at the moment.
NB: Yes.
Patrick: This is a sort of tradition that has grown up over the years and there are studies . . . which show that it is a waste of time. They collect nothing.
NB: So why are we wearing the masks, then?
Patrick: I haven't made the emotional change yet.

I pressed him about it later and he explained further.

Patrick: It's tradition. There is an element of ritual. I think that when you've had something so ingrained over your training and your practice, it's quite difficult to change . . .
NB: So do you feel that actually robing up, the ritual you go through, the putting on of the mask is an important element in fixing your psychological state of preparation? It's a sort of going into that special situation?

Patrick: I've never thought of it in those terms but I'm sure you're absolutely right. You get yourself mentally prepared.

Men are meaning-makers, in that they constantly use objects to create regular worlds around them. Even the colour of the gowns seems to have got drawn into it:

NB: I notice people here are wearing blue. I was told it was only ladies who wore blue and we should be careful to wear green. Is that right?
Patrick: Um, yes, I think it does seem to be right. I don't know whether they have worn out their clothes quicker and have gone on to the new blue stock.

Surgeons are closely watched by patients and small differences in their behaviour will be interpreted as omens of their own path to recovery or otherwise.

Patrick: In the ward she [the patient] will be near the entrance to the ward because that's where most of the nurses are for most of the time . . . and she'll get promoted up the ward as she recovers . . . People do, I think, know that as they progress up the ward they're getting nearer home, they're getting better. If you go the other way, you've got to start worrying.

Operating theatres, incidentally, are not the strained, severe places we might expect. Like undertakers' shops and murder trials, behind the scenes they can be riots of hilarity.

Patrick: If the surgeon and the theatre sister have got a sense of humour, a good sense of humour, that will become apparent as the afternoon or morning progresses. Provided people know when you're tense and it's time to shut up, the rest of the time it's quite nice to be relatively relaxed.

77

But just as life can be carved up into autonomous domains, so too can aspects of the same person. For example, one might expect that a surgeon would be totally untroubled by bloodshed. Not so.

Patrick: I'm terribly squeamish. We used to keep
chickens. One of the reasons we got rid of them was because
I couldn't bear the thought of wringing the chickens' necks.

It is clear that both our doctors are performers. For Patrick Jeffrey, one of the great attractions of his profession is that it continually allows him to monitor his own performance, both in front of his colleagues in the theatre, where he is the soloist, and before patients on ward rounds. Then, of course, there is gratitude.

Patrick: One of the great satisfactions of the job is going
round either to out-patients or to the ward, and people are
saying, 'Thank you.' I think it is probably one of the best
bits of the whole of the job. I love it.

Sue Campion-Smith remarked on a similar phenomenon amongst medical friends in Scotland, saying that they were treated 'like royalty'.

Patrick Jeffrey makes a deferential nod towards eschewing power over the patients.

Patrick: The family make the judgements about what you
should do and what you shouldn't. You just have to lead
them in the way their judgement's going to be made.
NB: But so great is your authority and so great is the
aura of confidence that surrounds you that you use the
word 'lead'. Is there a great deal of space for them to actually
decide?
Patrick: I hope there's enough space left that if they

78

wanted to go down the alternative route, they could feel free to do so. The door is open, but maybe it's not a very big door.

The point is, of course, that to be ill still involves a surrender of control over oneself. One is 'under the doctor'. Hospitals reduce us again to the status of infants who do not, according to the English view, own their own bodies. We are told when to eat, get up and go to bed. In fact, hospitals have an obsession with making us to go bed even when we are perfectly mobile, controlling our routine with harsh uniformity, removing our clothing and deliberately restricting our identity. Even the medical account of our illness traditionally belongs not to us, but to the hospital, which restricts access to the file containing it. A similar system obtains amongst certain Australian aboriginal peoples, where the story of a man's illness may not even be told by himself since it belongs to another.

Working Definitions

Jim Batchelor, my native informant, having observed all these variations on the themes of health and illness, saw no need to depart from his view of the body as a car. As long as it went, he was unconcerned about it. When it broke down, he went to a doctor to get it mended.

NB: Do you, for example, go to the doctor when you have a cold?
Jim: No, no. When I can't do me job.

From discussion, it is clear that most of Jim's notions about his body centre on work. When he is well, he can work. When he is

79

unable to work, that is the sign that he is *really* ill. It is his job that tells him how to see what may be happening to his body.

Back to Nature

It was the time of the Weymouth carnival, so Jim and I made our way to the beach. It was clear from the extraordinary operations on display there that for us nakedness is not 'natural', but a special state. People were engaging in all manner of furtive undressings, desperately looking around in fear. Others had brought bell tents of cloth inside which they could undress. Everywhere people were staring and picking at their own bodies, astonished to confront their own shoulders and hairy big toes. Rules of touching and even looking were being renegotiated. People were pulling bits of their bodies in or hiding themselves. For our culture, the desirable body is the young, even teenage, body, so that for most of our lives we are out of sympathy with our own form.

At the far end of the beach raged the carnival, people in extraordinary states of undress or transvestite display. Even for the English, bodies can be fun and restrictions on them relaxed to create a period of raucous bad taste, when anything goes. There abounded a sort of humour of the body with the erotic content of a knobbly-knees competition where the hideous and the unbecoming were positively sought after as in some punk anti-aesthetic. Yet in the midst of it sat the vacuously beaming beauty queen. The gamut of possible cultural attitudes to the body was completed by a WRAC band. Stern-faced, scrubbed women in uniform played martial music on brass instruments. Military organizations extend bodily control to extremes, so that the way the arms are swung, the turning of the head, the walk all become devoid of personal content. They remove hair and make-up, control moustaches and facial expression. For control of the body is an index of social control more generally. People whose hair or sexuality is out of control are felt to be capable of *anything.*

4 Giving up the Ghost

What people will believe is the measure of what they have to endure.
      Peter de Vries, *Slouching towards Kalamazoo.*

WESTERN SOCIAL SCIENCE has never been very good at coping with religion. To the believer, the explanation for belief is obvious: he believes what he does simply because it is true. Only to the unbeliever does the pernicious tenacity of faith without apparent foundation call for special justification. Normally, in the social sciences, religion has been dissected and explained in terms of something else. It is found to act as a form of social control, or to reinforce group solidarity, or – at a personal level – to comfort the oppressed through the hope of a better life to come or simply to provide the intellectual satisfaction of an ultimate cause. Hence the force of the remark by Peter de Vries quoted above.

In a single television programme it is impossible to deal with the enormous issues raised by the sociology of religion or the rationality debate, or even to give an accurate picture of religious life in England. We chose, then, to focus on three cults – the Church of England, a spiritualist church and the relatively new Jesus Army – and to try to show the enormous variety of religious activity in an apparently secular society.

The curious fact remains that most of us experience an increasing religious content in our ritual life as we progress through our earthly existence. While relatively few people are baptized, rather more are married in church and almost all undergo a funeral with explicit religious content. Traditionally it requires positive effort, an almost cranky determination, *not* to die a Christian. We decided, therefore, to focus on death as a point that would be likely to reveal important beliefs of ordinary people in relation to both official religious dogma and everyday social life.

The Church of England

The Church of England is our oldest nationalized industry. It enters into all aspects of the national civic religion, providing suitable rituals for public occasions. Thus it is the Church of England that performs the coronation of the monarch in the transfer of civil power and the magical continuity of royalty. It traditionally superintends the great Remembrance Day ceremonies that stress the harmony of the war dead, the living and the religion of peace. Such a role is generally analysed within sociology as that of 'legitimizing the social order'. It is interesting that there have been recent signs of strain between the national Church and political leaders, the former being reluctant to view the Falklands War victory as due to divine sponsorship of national aims. Politically, the Church of England has been viewed both as 'leftish' and as 'the Conservative Party at prayer'. In fact, its clergy seem to embrace a remarkable diversity of contradictory political opinions. In England nominal affiliation with the Church of England is customary. On government forms, as at the undertaker's, to describe oneself as C of E is to occupy an unmarked religious position that brings no expectation of any religious beliefs whatever.

The particular church we went to was St Martin's-in-the-Bull-ring, the parish church of Birmingham. It seems an apt symbol of the changing position in which the Church now finds itself. Although an ancient edifice, it now stands surrounded by roaring traffic on three sides and the seedy shopping centre of the Bullring on the other. Its lawns are no longer a graveyard but a sort of public space, the haunt of scavenging pigeons and winos. A warden on the door tactfully sorts the wheat of worshippers from the chaff of the drunk and disruptive. As a church, it is unusual in having no natural parish. Worshippers may drive from the suburbs on Sundays. Attempts are made to appeal to shoppers and workers by a midday communion service. We spoke to John Wesson, the vicar of the church.

John is some 50 years old and has been a clergyman for twenty-three years. He has been at St Martin's now for three years. The English clergy has developed its own form of oral delivery, fruity yet determinedly dispassionate, firm yet judiciously inexplicit. His response to my queries on the official view of life after death provides a good example.

John: It's very difficult to sum up the party line on something as mysterious as life after death, but certainly life continues after death – that God has purposes beyond our earthly life for us. And, of course, for Christians, the resurrection of Jesus Christ is one of the big articles of faith and that's always been the source of hope and comfort to Christians in times of bereavement and death – that because Christ conquered death, so there's something beyond for those who follow Christ and are part of his people, as it were. So I would be hesitant to say *exactly* what it was like beyond death, but that basic hope of resurrection and life beyond is very central to Christian teaching . . . You'll find some Christians who may be very dogmatic and argue this and that based on perhaps one or two verses of the Bible. But I suspect that a large number of Christians would hesitate to be too dogmatic, simply because it's a very mysterious area – that we're in our faith told some things but don't want to be too dogmatic about something from which people don't return to tell us the truth.

NB: Isn't it rather strange that Christianity doesn't have a firmer vision of what to offer us, in that it is one of the great attractions of Christianity, this hope of some future existence?

John: Well, I think it is a firm vision in the sense that we say Christ has risen, we go to be where Christ is, we believe God has a perfect future beyond the imperfections of suffering and pain in this world and those are precise in one sense, but if one starts talking in rather crude terms about 'What is Heaven like?' or 'What will we be doing, playing harps?' and those kind of images, that's, I think, where I begin to get a little bit uncertain and not keen to go down that road.

To an anthropologist, this seems suddenly very familiar – the problem of models and their relation to external reality, the limits of legitimate extrapolation from our own restricted experience. Indeed, the refusal to speculate beyond a certain point, not on grounds of dogma but because of paucity of data, recalls a scientific rather than a religious framework. (John Wesson, after all, has a degree in chemistry as well as theology.) Yet it is quite striking that the Church of England has no model of paradise to offer. The absence of a dominant folk model – Heaven as a perpetual wife-swapping party or a lifetime on the beaches of Torremolinos – suggests that it plays little part in active religion. Paradise nowadays is rather firmly defined by the English. It is a tropical island, as expressed in the fantasies of holiday brochures. It has beaches and palm trees. It is a place of no labour, where tropical exuberance delivers up the fruits of the soil without effort. It offers a life of natural simplicity away from the evils of culture. But few expect to go there *after* death and most see themselves excluded not by sin but by poverty.

Many Europeans who work in Third World countries are shocked to find that a religion is regarded as essential to all mankind bar the viciously criminal and the hopelessly insane. In such places to describe yourself as a Christian is not to use a mere euphemism for godlessness. You will frequently be consulted on religious matters as if an expert on the subject. The concerns of other cultures make you realize that Christianity is a very odd religion, indeed.

Its principal symbol, the cross, is an instrument of torture and violent death. In one of the areas in which I worked Christian converts had substituted for it the forked tree trunk beneath which enemies were beheaded so that their deaths could increase the fertility of men and the fields. None of the advertising experts in chapter 2 would have had anything to do with the cross as a badge. It would not sell. Yet, like all core symbols, it collapses many meanings together: the suffering of Christ, the triumph over death, the defeat of evil, the power of self-sacrifice, the hundreds of contexts of blessing and prayer in which we encounter it in the course of growing up in our community. It has an inherently paradoxical aspect, somewhat like the Dunkirk disaster of the Second World War – an appalling defeat that was somehow turned round and used as a symbol of inevitable victory. Indeed, the main function of the cross is to knit together strands of significance between all these and actively destroy analytical meaning to become the symbol of Christianity itself.

The act of communion has also been the source of libraries of interpretation. It centres, of course, on the notion of giving – Christ giving himself to God (who is also himself) for Man, who is giving bread and wine and money and receiving grace from God. The priest is the focus and alternately or simultaneously giver and receiver and the channel of communication. Yet communion has proved infinitely difficult as an idea. In some versions of Christianity the bread and wine in some sense actually become the body and blood of Christ; in others, the identification is mere symbolism; in yet others, the whole rite simply commemorates something that really happened only once in the past. In the nineteenth century in parts of West Africa its message was perceived as being dangerously close to cannibalistic rites of the traditional, local religion that the Church was trying to stamp out. For Christians, cannibalism is the very essence of heathen darkness and primitive wickedness, to which their own Church is opposed. Even today 'primitives' are depicted by the English as engaging in the eating of human flesh and intending field-workers are jocularly warned against the possibility of ending up in the cooking pot. Again, there seems to be a paradox. I asked John for his view on the subject.

John: It's no cannibalistic rite in the Christian faith. What we eat at Holy Communion is bread and wine, recognizing that they are pictures to us, very important and powerful pictures, symbols of the body and blood of Christ because that's what he gave for us . . . and Holy Communion is, in some sense, a kind of reliving of that. It's the picture language of faith. There's a range of views and lots of great volumes have been written about it and there are some Christians of more Catholic persuasion than myself who would perhaps want to think of body and blood in a more realistic sense than perhaps I would.

NB: You regard it as a purely symbolic statement. It is 'like', 'as it were'?

John: Yes, I think that the reality of Holy Communion is an inward spiritual experience.

One detects, here, the deep distrust of Protestantism for ritual and its power to effect change in the world. It is deeply reflected in the analyses that Protestant anthropologists have made of other religions. (The best-known anthropological studies of other religions were done by Catholic researchers.) Attempts by the peoples represented in ethnographic texts to control the weather or disease by non-scientific means are constantly interpreted by ethnographers as 'symbolic statements'.

When this does not work, the next ploy is to claim that rituals should be seen not as acting on the outside world but as affecting the psychological state of participants – like the surgeon's mask. Thus rituals that the locals tell you make it rain do not *really* make it rain, they stress the social importance of rain, or make people feel the dependence of the whole community on rain, or give a sense of control over thirst.

The Trinity, the fundamental unity of God, Christ and Holy Ghost, again confounds meaning. In a sense this is because Christianity is a religion quite literally designed by a committee, the result of endless attempts at harmonization and rationalization by Church councils over many centuries. Yet the Trinity looks very much like a skewed version of an act of primal incest such as underlies many origin myths all over the world. The mother is impregnated by the father, who is also the son.

The problem is shunted to one side by the insistence that such matters are 'mysteries' that Man should not expect to understand. They defy logic and require faith.

> *John:* I suppose one has to say that it is the mystery of
> God and that none of us ever think that we are going to be
> able to tabulate and pigeon-hole God with our human minds,
> so that at the end of the day we are left with a kind of
> incomprehensible fudged area and we are not ashamed of it.
> *NB:* So basically what you're saying is that we should
> believe in it, but not necessarily know what it means?
> *John:* I think we must believe in it. We must do our best
> to understand what it means within our limits, but I think
> what I'm saying is that I don't believe I, or anybody else,
> will fully grasp its depth and the fullness of it.

The recent history of the Church of England includes a sustained confrontation with Western science, leading to its retreat from all areas of falsifiable statements about reality. Shears of relevance, interpretation and context have been heavily wielded to limit those points where the two give contesting interpretations of the world. Their relationship is nowadays presented as being merely complementary or as one of a difference of levels.

These discussions of dogma, it should be said, were my obsession rather than John Wesson's, for St Martin's-in-the-Bullring stresses its concern with local social issues and sets heavy store by pastoral care of the community.

> *John:* I think that the way in which the Church is socially
> involved or political . . . is the continuing day-to-day ordinary
> pastoral ministry of the Church. It's an attempt to meet

ordinary human need with the reality of God and faith and so on. What the Church is aware of, and surely rightly, is that you can't simply talk about those things without addressing the real structural needs of the community in which we live, and I think we have become more vocal. If we want our faith to be taken seriously, we have to show how it touches upon every aspect of life. We don't think God is simply trapped in the church. He's the God who made the world, so he cares about all the things that are going on in the world and so we have some responsibility to be dealing with these and to be having our say and putting in our action at different points in all these areas . . . We have a lot of problems with homeless, alcoholics and so on, and these are all areas in which St Martin's willy-nilly is involved.

St Martin's traditionally has links with the market that surrounds it. As Markets Chaplain, the Reverend Nick Benson has special responsibility for these.

Nick: I think the purpose of a church like St Martin's, stuck in the middle of a city, is really to be dealing with the people who are using the city, the people who are working here, people who are passing through. It doesn't make sense for St Martin's to think of itself purely as a Sunday church. The only justification for us being here is what we do during the week.
NB: And you spend a lot of time actually going out and meeting people rather than waiting for them to come to you?
Nick: Oh yes. I mean, again, people do use the church, people do come in and pour through . . . but a lot of people don't have the chance to do that and so we need to get out more and see the traders, for instance. People like the traders are never going to be able to get to a normal service because

during the week, during the working day, they're busy, at least they're tied to a stall.

Also, one might note, most would not come anyway. With recent changes in population, about 80 per cent of them are Muslims. Nowadays the possession of a British passport brings no necessary implication of C of E membership.

We tried to sum up the parish with John:

NB: It seems a very 'uncosy' sort of parish.
John: It's a very uncosy parish, yes, yes. The most uncosy parish I've ever worked in, but, to that extent, so exciting and vibrant. One feels, day by day, that one's meeting the needs, the real needs, of men and women passing the door.

The emphasis here is probably significant. The Church of England is seen humanistically, as meeting *human* not *divine* needs. Just as social problems tend to be 'medicalized', so the Church has ceased to be sociologically naive and has been, to some degree, 'sociologized'. Sociological analyses in terms of latent functions, needs, social relevance have been taken back on board and affected the way the Church sees itself and justifies its own endeavours. Inevitably, they involve the notion that religion is *really about something else.*

At the moment we have before us a good example of the relationship between the Church of England and its cultural context: the problem of women. By slow degrees, the Church is moving towards the ordination of women as priests. The innovation is not without opponents among the male clergy. Yet as our notions of Man/Woman change, so do our notions of God. Sexual symbolism of an explicit kind – not the Freudian version that sees a penis in every spire and womb in every crypt – is rife within Christianity. Christ is the (male) bridegroom of his (female) Church, which sprang from the side of Christ like Eve from Adam. Nuns are the brides of Christ, which leaves monks and priests in a doubtful position. However one views communion, it seems that at some point an identification has to be made between priest and Christ as the mediator linking God and Man.

An argument exists that since Christ was male, and because his relation to the Church is male, a woman's sexuality debars her from representing him. Curiously, it is not argued that since all the disciples partaking in the original communion meal were male, women should be debarred from this. It is really an argument about what is *essentially* feminine. The paradox is that views about essential femininity are always culture-bound and therefore change. The debate has not come about because of theological changes. Change is coming from outside the Church because our views on the nature of women have changed.

The Reverend Sue Summers, also of St Martin's-in-the-Bull-ring, talked to us about it. Sue is 28 years old and married to a clergyman. She was ordained as a deaconess in 1986, but when the rules changed in 1987 she became a deacon.

Sue: I was a deaconess once, which meant that I was
part of the laity of the Church of England. We all got
reordained as deacons. That has meant that I ceased to be a
member of the laity of the Church of England and I am now
a clergyperson, which is obviously a mixed blessing. It means
that the only thing I cannot do, I can't give the absolution
in the church service and to say the blessing in the church
service and to consecrate the bread and wine in the
Eucharist.
NB: So losing your suffix doesn't mean to say that you've
lost your sex. You're still very much a woman within the
ministry?
Sue: Absolutely, yes, and I think a lot of people were
frightened about that and a number of people actually spoke to
me and said, 'You're not going to wear a dog-collar, are you?' as
if they felt that would be really something they couldn't handle.

94

In fact, women in the clergy have adapted the uniform of the
Church rather in the same ways as schoolgirls and female
soldiers have modified the special dress of their own areas.
During the service Sue wears the same type of clothing as John.
Ecclesiastical garb, with its long robes, is not strongly marked as
male. For everyday wear, where a male might wear a suit with a
dog-collar, Sue has devised a frilly dress with a high front, in-
corporating a stretch of white dog-collar. It is not black, however,
but bright yellow.

Sue: Fewer people are obviously wearing black in the
Church and I don't see any reason why, if I don't want to, I
should, because part of what I bring to the ministry is my
person and my personality, and if I want to express that in
my clothes, then I shall do so.
NB: It doesn't bother you that people will say, 'Well,
this is proof that women are not serious about the ministry'
and that they're basically a little frivolous?
Sue: Oh, no, it doesn't bother me at all. That's their
problem . . . There are plenty of examples of women who
do wear black, or a lot of women who actually refuse to
wear a dog-collar at all because of the maleness of the
symbol.

Sue sees the problem of women in the ministry as simply part
of a very much deeper male bias in the Church.

Sue: Men have been throughout tradition the ones who
have formulated the doctrine, the ones who have reflected
upon Christ, the ones who have taught, so there's going to
be obviously a kind of bias and their own problems or hang-
ups are going to come through that.

Basic, of course, is the notion of 'God the Father'.

Sue: How my view of God has to be depends on my

experience of him and I pray because I get to know him
better and obviously I reflect upon Jesus. But for me it has
to be a mother *and* a father for warmth and softness, and
the maternal imagery is very important to me.
NB: But that notion of man as the authority figure and
the female as the soft, cherishing figure, that's rather from
our culture . . .
Sue: Oh, yes, very much so. Well, I'm a product of a
stereotype culture as much as anyone else is, so obviously
I'm going to be discovering that too. I think in other cultures
God is perceived in very different ways.

Elsewhere in the Church of England another figure has staged
something of a comeback, the Virgin Mary.

Sue: I think maybe that's pointing towards an awareness
of the insufficiency of the male model of God, in that we –
that some people – need to have this female, Mary, who is a
very strong mother image . . .
NB: So our image of God is changing to bring it in line
with our image of male and female in the outside world?
Sue: Yes, yes. People are bringing their own experiences
to faith and may be finding that what they experienced
doesn't fit with what they've been told.

Yet the Virgin Mary, too, is subject to constant reinterpreta-
tion.

NB: She's a bit of a wimp in many ways, isn't she?
Sue: Oh, no. I disagree. Oh, in tradition perhaps, but as
we find her in the Bible, I don't think she's a wimp at all.
For me she is the model of somebody who is able to say Yes
to God and I see her as a very powerful figure because, for
me, in the Annunciation, when the angel came and said,
'Would you do this?', for me, the whole of salvation hung

in the balance in that moment, because she could have said, 'No, thanks.'

If God made Man in his image, then Man has returned the compliment with a vengeance.

The Jesus Army

The Jesus Army is the 'rescue army' of the Jesus Fellowship Church, a Baptist church that experienced a strong revival in the 1960s. The world religions are a rich soup out of which different groups can fish any parts that appeal to them. The Jesus Army homes in on notions of community and sharing. It deliberately seeks out the socially deprived, what it terms 'the forgotten people'. One of its advertisements runs:

> Ex-con, rentboy, prostitute, homeless, in debt, run-away, on drugs – it doesn't matter how bad your scene. We want to help you!

The Army offers food and accommodation within its communities in the hope of saving the afflicted.

We went out evangelizing on the streets of Birmingham with the Army. A specially converted bus, with facilities for producing infinite quantities of tea, served as the battlewagon. Liz Donovan, a member of the movement, told us about it.

> *Liz:* It's our hand of outreach to the needy, to those who are trapped in various forms of social evils and it is the heart of the Church that feels concerned at the state of the nation . . . We see a real need to bring God back into the nation. Every member of the Jesus Army has had an

97

experience, conversion experience, experience of God and as a result of that, we are very grateful people.

The bus was full of young people, teenagers, those in their twenties and early thirties. Community singing of a religious nature and to the accompaniment of guitars was a constant element. It was explained to me that this was to express the joy of the community.

NB: Why is the community so important?
Liz: Jesus spoke about justice and equality. Living in a Christian community is one of the easier ways . . . because we are a Church which is a community, in fact, pools all its possessions.
NB: Absolutely everything?
Liz: Everything. Therefore you are able to live equally. We are able to live a simple life-style. We are able to let every area of our life be devoted to brethren and to God.

Although residence in a community is not essential, some two-thirds of the members do live in this way. Some work outside the community in normal paid jobs and contribute their entire earnings to a central kitty. Others work inside the community, which also owns businesses, such as a health-food shop. In such a system identity through possessions becomes an impossibility. Great stress is placed on love.

Liz: There are many hundreds of people who we help just in a human way, just in terms of from one human being to another. They may never join the Church. They may never come and stay with us.

But this is very much *not* erotic love. Indeed, the Army is quite keen on allotting separate spheres to male and female. Sex is one of the ways the Devil can get at you. Celibacy is held to be a 'good thing'.

> *Liz:* I'm celibate. I found the cost of celibacy, in other
> words the cost of devoting myself to God without being
> married, something to be considered very seriously. I'm
> thrilled to be celibate now. I find it extremely fulfilling and it
> gives me the freedom to devote myself more fully to the
> Church.

Celibacy, of course, is not unknown elsewhere in the Christian world. It is an interesting use of denial of sexuality as a denial of self, the avoiding of the fleshly material in the interests of the spirit. In a world where everything was shared, its only alternative would be free love, an option known in other religious communes.

The singers set up in the heart of Birmingham's Bullring and sang lustily with apparent enjoyment, attracting a small crowd, not all of whom fled on being approached by other members of the Army. Members are recognizable by the wearing of a uniform. In the case of the men this is a sort of camouflage jacket with the sleeve badge, 'We fight for you.'

> *NB:* What sort of reaction do you normally get?
> *Liz:* Oh, you get everything. You get people who say as
> much as 'Leave me alone' as you get people who are
> interested and those who are not, but I think you probably
> get more who are not today . . . There is in people sometimes
> a switch-off on religion as well.
> *NB:* Yes. It's also a very unEnglish thing to literally wear
> Jesus on your sleeve, isn't it?
> *Liz:* Yes, yes, it is. I think we're very reserved in England
> and it's almost a little bit taboo to talk about God and
> things that are very personal. I mean, you can have people
> say they don't wish to discuss it because it's private.

Most of the people seemed very polite but unenthusiastic. Two of the young men of the Army told me they had found a man drunk and asleep on a bench and prayed for him. Because he did not wake up, they left a note saying they had prayed for him. They prayed for me too. The Army has a strong belief in the external and direct efficacy of prayer in a fashion that would be distrusted by the Church of England. The Reverend Sue Summers, for example, remarked that she would not expect God to interfere in the course of an illness by curing, but rather by giving strength to the afflicted in his suffering. Again, the effect of 'ritual' is seen to be on the psyche, *not* the outside world. The Jesus Army, on the other hand, do not distance themselves from real implications with long tongs of rationality and expect a very personal knowledge of God through a religious experience. Liz told us about hers.

> *Liz:* My family had brought me up to fairly good standards. At that point I completely turned against my upbringing. I thought. 'I want everything this world has to offer.' That's where I went for the jet set and started climbing. Now in the midst of that I met this girl who talked to me about Jesus. I felt convicted . . . So I thought about this for a while and one night, shortly after hearing this message, I was by myself. I was trying to go to sleep and I experienced God drawing nearer. I can only express it in that way. I experienced a warmth around, drawing near to me almost causing me to choose. To choose him or to choose the life I had. It was like a choice. It was like the power of love saying, 'Choose me. That's the way to life, the fullness of life, or carry on in your way of sin.' And at that point the reality of it became very clear to me and I chose it, a little bit reluctantly, but I chose it. I said, 'OK, God. I choose you.'
>
> *NB:* So what did you do?
>
> *Liz:* At that point?
>
> *NB:* Yes.
>
> *Liz:* I immediately fell asleep.

Liz's account bears the marks of an account smoothed by repetition. One imagines that recounting one's conversion experience is a regular part of Jesus Army life.

Despite the Jesus Army's stress on the reality of God and prayer, its attitude to the sacraments is curiously 'symbolic'.

> *Liz:* At least once a month we break the bread and share wine, on a Sunday morning when the whole Church gathers together. At least a thousand members gather together . . .
> We also do it on a Tuesday evening. Our Tuesday evening is called our agape [love] meal and that's an evening which is quite a special evening for us. We gather together as a sort of representation of our commitment to God and our commitment to one another, so it's a meal to which you wouldn't invite visitors, nor would you miss. Jesus says break bread and share wine in remembrance of him, so it's a good thing to be remembering what he has encouraged. It's an expression of our life together. It's something that's ongoing and so, therefore, say, you've fallen out with somebody, or you need to forgive someone, it's there you do it before you take bread and wine.
> *NB:* Within the established Church, of course, it's only a priest who can break the bread and bless the wine . . .
> *Liz:* That's not common, I think, to all Christianity. Anybody can break bread and share the wine. Although normally you'd have leaders who would, at the head of the table, break the bread and share it.

Visions of life after death, too, are inevitably informed by our experience in this life. For the Jesus Army, life in Heaven will be communal.

Keeping in Touch

The last sect that we looked at was the National Spiritualist Union. It claims a membership of some three-quarters of a million and runs 350 churches (or 'centres') all over the country. Eric Hatton is in the stationery business and is also a minister of the National Spiritualist Union. Elderly, professorial and very middle-class, he was not what I had expected. Spiritualism in my part of London tends to mean the ecstatic religions of West Indian sects. At the service we attended in Stourbridge the congregation were overwhelmingly female and elderly, middle-class and white. The proceedings were extremely decorous.

Before the service, we had the opportunity to talk to Eric about his beliefs. Since the Church centres on establishing a bridge between this life and a future existence, it is not, perhaps, surprising that it has firmer notions on the next world than the established Church.

> *Eric:* I have established, for my own satisfaction, that life after death is a fact and that people, when they die, no matter what their belief may be, whether they have faith of any order or not, *scientifically* they survive and that survival is not something that is dependent upon some latter day, but it is almost an instantaneous thing. When the physical body has terminated its life-energy-giving forces, the spiritual body gradually draws away and enters into a new dimension.

Coming from an Anglican background, Eric cites biblical precedent for encounters with the spirits of the dead.

> *NB:* So you would regard yourself as still a Christian?
> *Eric:* Not in that sense. My difference would be that I am not anti-Christian . . . We subscribe to the fact that Jesus was

a most gifted, sensitive prophet, seer, healer . . . But whereas
the Christian Church tended to emphasize that only by belief
in Jesus can you be saved . . . I believe that a God who is
behind everything within the universe does not pronounce
in favour of Christianity any more than he does of Judaism.

Again, it is direct experience that is given as the clinching
element of faith.

Eric: I had some smatterings of evidence . . . but I think
the breakthrough that finally convinced me and my family,
who were by no means open to conviction, was the fact
that, when my brother, who crashed into the sea on his last
sortie in the St Paul area, communicated with us through a
medium he gave us outstanding evidence of his serial
number in its correct order, of his rank, of his two names,
and also of his nickname, which only my sister and I used
to use. But more than that, he related little details which
would only be known, I believe, to my mother, my father,
my sister and me, and those were the things that would
cement one's belief that people who are communicating with
us are, in fact, the people who they claim to be.

So what is this existence like? What of Heaven and Hell? Eric
is a little vague on these points. The problem is that communication requires a sensitive medium. It is those on the other side
who must wish to communicate with us and not vice versa.
Hence, all one has is glimpses. It is varied, sometimes good,
sometimes bad. There is some form of segregation of the wicked.

Eric: People who have been bad people in this life, murderers,
tormentors, you name it, those who have contributed toward
the things that we all abhor in this society of ours are
obviously not compatible in a state of being that decent, kindly,
generous, loving people live in and it seems that the separation

is simply because of the natural laws that are universal, and therefore life on the other side is a very varied experience.

The service itself was modelled on conventional Christian forms, with hymns and prayers, though clearly without the customary allusions to Christ. The hymn-book proclaimed belief in a single high god, 'subject to interpretation'. God was referred to as 'The great power of our universe, who we call both father and mother God'. The highpoint for all, however, was clearly the 'clairaudient', Gordon Higginson. Gordon is President of the National Spiritualist Union and has a considerable following in spiritualist circles. The church was packed. Hopes and expectations were high.

Gordon began by producing a name or a set of initials. A member of the congregation would claim them. This would be followed up by further information that the claimant would assent to or deny. A standard example would be, 'You have recently passed through some kind of an anniversary.' Almost always the audience member would concur. Then would come a message mixed with further information such as, 'This lady is trying to get to her daughter.' Assent would gain further information, 'She is talking about your father. I would think that your father must be passed over.' Assent. 'You have known a family named Hill?' Assent. Denial of a piece of information could often be explained by similarity of sound with another word or the fact that 'That's the name of the lady who usually sits in this seat' or 'That's my friend beside me.' Messages were given as if passed over a crowded, noisy channel. Messages were always of comfort: 'You will overcome.' (Gordon later revealed in private that spiteful and angry messages *do* occur but he never passes them on.) Typically they refer to meetings with deceased friends or give thanks to wives who nursed them faithfully. Often, they are staggeringly explicit. 'You have three plants in your house and one belonged to this lady.' 'You have a small round table inherited from your mother.' 'There is something about Switzerland but you won't be going.' 'They always called you Mom – not Mam or Mum – but Mom.' 'Arthur

asks, "Did the trousers fit?"' (Reply: 'No, I had to turn them up.')
Almost always, Gordon is declared to be absolutely correct.

English people I have talked to about the session have always
questioned me eagerly about how it could have been 'fixed',
looking for loopholes, asking about the self-deception of communicants, the degree to which Gordon's remarks address themselves
to public knowledge. The fact that Gordon would sometimes
confuse people sitting close to each other, or those who habitually
sat in a certain seat with present occupants, was interpreted by
some as evidence of fakery, by others as signs of a genuine,
disturbed communication. Others again were prepared to accept
Gordon as a mind-reader but not a clairaudient. Perhaps such a
performance could have been arranged in advance, though at
enormous cost. I had little doubt at the time about the up-
rightness of those involved. The history of psychic investigation
is, of course, dotted with deliberate and unconscious deception.
The important thing for me remains the pragmatic attitude of
the congregation to matters that, for the national Church, are
mysterious by definition and doubtful in experience. One does
not expect to see everything one believes nor believe everything
one sees. Such decisions are taken in advance.

Many of the communicants were reduced to tears, but not
necessarily of sadness. There is no doubt that they derived deep
consolation from these messages and that the congregation was
sent away uplifted and genuinely comforted. There was no doubt
that for most this was a firm demonstration of life after death.
For them, this was not a matter of faith but of clear evidence.

I asked Eric how his belief that life continues 'over the other
side' had affected the way he felt about death.

NB: Your faith in this spiritual dimension of life, does it
mean that, for you at least, death has truly lost its sting?
Eric: Absolutely, yes. I often say to my friends and children
that if anything happened to me tomorrow, it would not

concern me. But I must admit that I have a great love for my wife and my children and my grandchildren and many friends and I would regret leaving them, but that is a purely personal thing, as I think they would regret my leaving them. But the fact that I know that our separation is but of a short duration and we surely . . . shall meet again . . . that is something which I think should enhance life for everyone.

The Sting of Death

We would be committing an error if we entirely attributed this flight from death to an indifference toward the dead person. In reality, the contrary is true. In the old society the panoply of mourning scarcely concealed a rapid resignation. How many widowers remarried a few short months after the death of their wives!

On the contrary, today, where mourning is forbidden, it has been noted that the mortality rate of widows or widowers during the year following the spouse's death is much higher than that of the control groups of the same age.*

There is a void left by the established Church, which doggedly refuses to offer a clear picture of what happens at death. As one cleric remarked to me, 'Purgatory? Judgement? The resurrection of the dead at the Last Trump? No, we don't really have a clear

* Philippe Aries, *Western Attitudes toward Death from the Middle Ages to the Present*, Baltimore and London, Johns Hopkins University Press, 1974.

picture about all that. Perhaps the Catholics do.' Alongside a secular and materialist creed that determinedly refuses to consider the possibility of a life after death there has emerged in England a demotic faith outside the Church with a rich multiplicity of beliefs. Resurrection, ghostly revenants and reincarnation all find lively supporters amongst contemporary English believers. Perhaps this extra-ecclesiastical creed is nothing new and has always been there, flourishing in the shade of the official dogma. The sensational images of horror films that delight and terrify us on the cinema screen are only the commercialized tip of an iceberg of seriously held beliefs.

Not only the theology of death, but its very physical reality is deliberately obscured by our own culture. We talked to Don Moar, a senior funeral director in the Midlands and in charge of a business that handles some 8,000 cadavers a year. Don feels that the English regard death as 'one of the last taboos', but is cool and professional about his own work. He looks death in the face a dozen times a day.

NB: Do you own up to what you do for a living?
Don: Yes, I do now. When I was younger I didn't.

Nowadays almost everyone engages a funeral director to deal with death on their behalf. There is no legal obligation to do so, but any alternative is well on its way to becoming unthinkable. Funeral directors, moreover, are expanding their field of activity. Most have 'viewing chapels', where relatives may come and 'view' the dead. This is relatively new, within the last ten or fifteen years. Previously, the dead would be exhibited in the front room, the room that presented the public façade of the family and was used only on formal occasions. As the front room has disappeared, so has the tradition of showing the body. Of course, death, too, has been 'medicalized' and usually occurs in hospital. The death-bed scenes of our forebears are a thing of the past. Should death occur in the home, the haste to remove the body is almost indecent.

NB: And people are quite keen to get the body out of the
house and into your chapel as soon as possible?
Don: Oh, yes. We offer a twenty-four-hour service. We
usually can respond within thirty minutes if people want
somebody moving and that's the usual order of the day. It's
very occasionally they want them back home, very rare.

Indeed, in England we so arrange things that many people
may never see a dead body. I had certainly never seen one before
working in Africa, where they are a disconcerting part of everyday reality.

NB: I presume the majority of people have never seen a
dead body before.
Don: That's right and with a bit of luck you'll go through
life without ever seeing one as well because not everybody
wants to come and view. In the days when they were in the
front parlour, everybody went, all had to go to pay their
respects. But we know from the rate of viewing not very
many people do . . . Fewer and fewer – and fewer and fewer
people attend funerals.

Don sums up his job as 'to make the whole thing disappear',
'the public don't really want to know'. The most awkward
period seems to be that between the death and the service, a sort
of limbo where everyone is waiting for a formal punctuation
mark to finalize death. One of the many things the public are
unclear about is 'hygienic preparation'. Since this is a standard
practice, most bodies in England undergo it whether it is re-
quested or not.

NB: What exactly does 'hygienic preparation' involve?
Don: Preservation, which is to delay the onset of
decomposition, which obviously will happen; and
presentation, which is to give the deceased a more relaxed

appearance, which is obviously more pleasing to the
relatives . . .
NB: You actually remove the blood?
Don: That's right, yes, and that is replaced with a
preservative.
NB: It sounds very *unhygienic*.

In an unwittingly vampire-like fashion, the preservative is
pumped into one neck artery, forcing the blood out of the other.
The fluid is massaged into finger ends and other extremities where
clotting blood may be causing a blue discoloration. Often, it will be
necessary to pierce the heart and abdomen to suck out accumulated
juices and release gas. In fact, although arguments about 'removing
risk of bacterial infection' are used to justify the practice, the use of
refrigerators and simple washing of the body would be equally
effective. As if to confirm Don's view of death as 'the last taboo', the
IBA refused to allow the pictures we took of this to be shown.

NB: Would you say that the principal reason for it is
cosmetic? That it makes the body look more like a living
person?
Don: That's right . . . That's going to be their last memory
of that person and their memory will be that little bit happier
perhaps, feeling that the deceased has arrived and is at peace
rather than as they last saw them, maybe in a traumatic
illness.
NB: So you're going for an image of someone asleep?
Don: That's right, yes. You can't deny that the person
has died, but let's show that they died in peace.

To complete the process of hygienic preparation, the jaws may
have been sewn together to prevent the mouth opening and the
hair will have been washed and blow-dried. Make-up may well
be applied and injuries or post-mortem incisions concealed. A
problem with bodies straight from a refrigerator is their tendency
to sweat.

109

The ceremony of 'viewing' fixes the relatives' final memory in ritual fashion. This corresponds to the photography of the wedding that 'fixes' the day and becomes the official memory of it. To take family photographs at an English funeral would, nowadays, be regarded as an appalling *faux pas*. The viewing chapels themselves express the role of the funeral director. The body is wheeled in from what is really a workshop with bright, fluorescent lighting and concrete floors. The chapel is a small room with dimmed lighting and religious images. Once this door is shut, the mourners enter through another door from an area of thick carpeting, muted light and paintings of the countryside showing the change of the seasons. A rigorous division is maintained between the front and the back, the public face and the reality.

Increasingly, the service is held at a crematorium. Transport will be chauffeur-driven, in the special hearse for the deceased (with or without flowers) and in special large black saloon cars for the mourners. 'We like a car with a boot,' explained Don. 'It adds dignity.' The undertaker's staff are impeccably turned out in black formal wear and must look suitably grave.

Don: Seventy per cent of all are actually cremations anyway and where people don't have a particular religious involvement, then they perhaps have the full service at the crematorium, but if they've had a long involvement with the Church, then, of course, they'll want to have the church service beforehand.
NB: Most people do want some sort of Church presence though, don't they?
Don: Yes, they do. Even if they've had no involvement with the Church. I know one or two of the vicars have often said that it's almost as though, you know, it wouldn't be done properly if you didn't have benefit of clergy. I think that's the British thing, isn't it? If anyone asks you what religion you are, you always say C of E if you haven't got any beliefs and people follow that through to the grave.

One curious ritual fact emerged.

Don: We always carry a coffin feet first, but a priest's
coffin will be placed head first, with his head to the altar.
NB: Do you know why that is?
Don: I suppose that's his rightful place, isn't it, facing the
congregation, rather than facing the altar as a layman would
be.

We went behind the scenes with Ken Elliott, manager of a
large crematorium, to see the part that the public don't. The
service is brief and deliberately bland. The chief images are those
of vegetable growth, homing in on the paradox that a seed
seems to die so that it can grow. The vicar explained to me that
he often left out the bits about the perishable and imperishable
as unnecessarily physical. Upstairs is the image of the seed that
dies only to germinate into new life; downstairs the machinery of
death is light industrial. The coffin descends through a square
hole to the accompaniment of organ music and disappears from
the mourners' sight.

Ken reveals that a great deal of thought has gone into that
final moment.

Ken: In Britain there's three methods of committal: one
would be this descending method; one would be a catafalque
that had doors that opened at the end, which would open at
the point of committal and the coffin would disappear; and
the third, which personally I dislike very much, is curtains
that come round and hide the coffin from the mourners. At
that point they say goodbye. I like [the descending method].
I think this has got earth burial about it. They're used to
seeing the coffin descend and one thing they can do, if they
want to, with this method is to actually gather round what
is virtually a grave . . .
NB: So this is a very important punctuation point?

Ken: I think it is, yes. It is the last point at which the
family mourners and friends say goodbye to someone who
has been very important to them.

The job of everyone at funerals is to make things go smoothly,
as if everything is happening by itself as a natural process. This
is sometimes taken very literally. The code of conduct governing
crematoria explicitly lays down that there should be no mech-
anical or friction noise.

Ken: Very important. For example, the catafalque we
have here is hydraulic. It comes down on gravity and is put
back by a motor. If there's anything wrong with the
hydraulics of this, then there may be the faintest sort of
sound like a slight groaning sound, which is the last thing
that you really want in a chapel at a service.

The coffin is then wheeled to the furnace, preheated with gas
to 450°C. Thereafter the coffin and body provide most of the fuel,
the operator controlling the amounts of air and gas fed into the
furnace. Contrary to popular belief, only one body is incinerated
at a time. After some ninety minutes, combustion is complete and
the ash, which contains some large pieces of bone and any odd
mementoes the mourners may have popped inside the coffin, is
transferred to the grinder to be reduced to a uniform grey powder.

NB: Why is that important?
Ken: I don't know. I think that it's just what's happened
somehow . . . In that sort of form – the bone form – they
would need to be buried rather than scattered . . . But I
somehow think that it has been happening for such a long
time that nobody has perhaps asked that question before.
NB: So maybe it's something to do with the complete
destruction of the body? The body has to be *completely*
destroyed.
Ken: Absolutely.

The next part is one of those curious aspects that crop up in English rituals, a sort of 'free play' area, like the means of transport of the bride. The disposal of the ashes becomes almost a challenge to the imagination. With the disappearance of family ties beyond one generation, the notion of the family vault is a thing of the past, though husband and wife may ask for their ashes to be scattered on the same spot. What do most people do with them?

> *Don:* Oh, all sorts of things. I mean, usually they're
> scattered in the garden of remembrance in the crematorium,
> but people do take them away in modern urns to keep on
> the mantelpiece, take them to the cricket ground, football
> ground or wherever was their favourite place, to be scattered.
> And we've even had the situation when somebody brought
> twelve matchboxes for the ashes to be spread between the
> boxes so that they could give one to each member of the family.

English funerals are a complex play on the notions of the impermanent and the eternal. Apart from 'hygienic preparation', there is no attempt to eternalize the body itself, yet the 'dirty' processes of decay will be cheated by incineration. No attempt either is made to sort the body into impermanent flesh and permanent bone, as is common in other cultures. Vegetal symbolism – the flowers (*Don: They add a bit of life*), the incorporation of ashes into the cycle of nature, the metaphors of the committal ceremony – are the only optimistic note hinting that decay and growth may be the same thing. Everything speaks of dissolution and the destruction of the individual. Yet there is a dogged insistence – in the face of copious evidence to the contrary – at both private funerals and the big public ceremonies of remembrance that the dead will not be forgotten, that they will live on as a memory. This finds its expression in attitudes to memorials.

NB: Do you think it's important for people to have some

memorial, or do people not worry so much about that these days?

Ken: I think there's a good mix of that. I think that in many ways, a large majority of bereaved love to have something tangible, something, in a way, to see, rather like a cemetery affords with its tombstones, somewhere to go.

The contrast between the public façade of the undertaker's and what happens behind it is maintained throughout the service at the crematorium and beyond.

NB: Now, it's very striking about this place that really the process is quite markedly industrial, yet the people will think of it as a garden of remembrance.

Ken: Yes . . . I think gardens in most people's minds are idyllic, peaceful places. I think people like gardens. I think they like the concept of the natural life in gardens and I think that if a garden . . . is the final resting place for somebody, I think a lot of people would be extremely happy with the thought of that.

NB: So people may have spent their lives in the city, but they all end up here, buried in the country, in a garden.

Ken: In a way, yes. At least in their mind . . .

In my experience English funerals are far from being a comforting event; they greatly intensify grief. Don trains young undertakers in the skills of dealing with grief.

Don: That's one of the aspects we cover in the course . . . It depends on the individual's own response to grief . . . the way in which grief manifests itself in them because it can have so many different ways of showing . . . like in aggression, anger, guilt . . .

NB: I was interested you mentioned guilt. I was talking to a priest the other day and he said, you know, we always

talk conventionally about grief but, in fact, a great deal of
what we call grief is guilt.
Don: That's right. Yes, people feel that perhaps they
should have done more . . . But we have a role in so far as
the funeral is the first step in the process of bereavement
and getting over the death. It's a ceremony that's saying,
'Right, this person has passed away, the funeral is now
taking place.'

Don sees funerals as primarily working on the living, bringing
out grief and expressing it. People require rituals to make clear
public statements about what has happened, to regloss the event
so that it can be fixed in the memory as something complete and
finished. This is the role of the established Church in the lives of
most of us. It has nothing to do with religion. English culture
provides a fixed ceremonial to cope with death and turn it into
theatre, but it is a ceremony with no obvious meaning and so
can be used by godly and ungodly alike. They must each fill it
with their own meaning.

This explains something of the obsession of the English with
recovering bodies after accidents or disasters. The burial is an
emotional low point, a punctuation mark, from which people
can move forward. If there is no body, it is impossible to hold a
funeral that allows you to move on. This is curious. Other
cultures regularly permit funerals without bodies.

There seems to be an odd tension in the English, a need for
ritual yet a deep distrust of it. Mourning has now ceased to be
a public display, therefore engaging in it smacks of affectation
and insincerity. The curtains of the house are not drawn, nor do
the family wear black or black armbands. It has become a private
matter involving that central core of emotional being, something
to be gone through tastefully at home.

The striking thing about the English notion of death is that it is
regarded as a totally negative thing, a form of social failure. There
is no real place for the dead in our lives. Mention of them provokes

embarrassment and apology. Unlike other cultures, we hardly have a notion of a 'good death'. The closest we come to such a concept is perhaps to be struck down in the midst of pleasure, an end that casts no shadow before it, that involves no reflection on the ultimate verities and interrupts life as little as possible. It might with justification be said that we do not just dispose of our dead, we throw them away and have no continuing relationship with them.

Jim Batchelor, my native informant, was quite clear that this was what he wanted.

Jim: I'll be cremated actually.

NB: But you're going to have a clergyman there?

Jim: Well, it's traditional and I suppose it's the normal thing to do, but I don't believe in the Church in a sense, no.

NB: But if you go first, your wife's going to go straight round there and get a clergyman?

Jim: Get the old insurance money and a clergyman, yes.

NB: Why do you want to be cremated, not buried? That's more traditional, isn't it?

Jim: Well, I think being buried really is a little bit selfish, in a sense, because you're in that little plot of ground and the wife or husband, whoever it is, is still bound to that bit of ground because they know your body's in there. Well, once you're cremated, that's it. It's finished and gone. That gives them the chance to start a new life.

NB: Oh, that's very interesting . . . That seems to be what a lot of traditional peoples feel; you know, once the body has gone, the husband or wife is free to go off and make a fresh start.

Jim: Yes, I believe that, that's what I like to believe. You've got your little memories, but that's how I look at it.

5 Time out of Time

We travel through time as through a country filled with many wild and empty wastes, which we would fain hurry over, that we may arrive at those several little settlements or imaginary posts of rest which are disposed up and down in it.

Joseph Addison, *Spectator*, 16 June 1711

THE ENGLISH VIEW time in spatial terms. Time flows in one direction. The future lies before us, the past behind us. Events are viewed as happening 'here', in between the two. So time, to us, is seen in terms of place. There is a feeling that in this space between past and future we are all prey to good and bad fortune and events beyond our own control. In the modern world we are no longer masters of our own destinies. Enmeshed in world economies, market forces and specialist knowledge to which we have no access, we feel ourselves wrenched about by external forces. These are the elements that generate our notion of 'news'.

We chop time up into standard units of hours, minutes and seconds, as measured by clocks, and use these to establish the zones that punctuate our regular existence. The normal day is, above all, structured by work. Working time creates its opposite, 'free time', which is our own and can be allocated as a scarce resource. Little, jealously defended islands of free time dot our lives – tea-breaks, lunch-hours, evenings. Longer free periods occur at weekends and, above all, holidays. We mark them off by our clothes, our activities, powerful little rituals like the first drink of an evening.

Holidays are structured among themselves. Christmas is traditionally a time for 'going home', a time of family and the hearth. A modern trend is to go abroad, but only to a more extreme *winter* climate in search of snow. Summer holidays are for 'going away', abroad, if possible, to a more extreme *summer* climate where everything around us signifies heat. To stay at home during this period can only be justified on grounds of extreme poverty. To stay at home is not to have a proper holiday at all. Through our movements we reproduce a more marked form of the local rotation of the seasons, turning changes of time into changes of place and magnifying them in our motions. So, within our notions of linear time that flows in one direction, there is room for cyclical time, the regular recurrence of the bench-marks of the year.

119

Holidays especially involve the exhilaration that comes from the abandonment of control, a time outside regular existence. We visited Great Yarmouth, a traditional holiday resort on the east coast, at the end of the summer season. Great Yarmouth caters for the 'family holiday', especially the working-class family. The Billington family are a youngish couple with two children, aged 9 and 11. Despite a bitter east wind and the threat of rain, they sat determinedly on the beach in anoraks.

> *NB:* Here you are on holiday. Why do you do it?
> *Mum:* Partly because we enjoy Great Yarmouth. We set
> off for the day and have a really good time. There's a really
> good market, the shops are good, the pleasure beach is nice
> . . . somebody else does all the cooking and cleaning and
> decides what we're having for meals . . . I can just sit back
> and eat when I'm ready and go out and enjoy myself in
> between.

The essence of the holiday, then, seems to be freedom from routine. Dad does not have to go to work, Mum is released from household routine, the children are freed from school. In such an existence, the only structuring device seems to be food, and meals are the fixed marks on which people hang their whole schedule. The one o'clock hamburger becomes a barrier against cosmic chaos.

It is difficult to get people to think about holidays. It is quite obvious to them that holidays are justified in terms of 'fun' and they are reluctant to look beyond such a word. But nothing varies more than the idea of what is self-evidently fun. 'Fun' usually implies a whole world view. Mum describes her idea of a holiday as the chance to 'bust off a bit, run a little bit wild' but only within limits, as is clear from her notion of going abroad.

> *Mum:* We can go out and let off a bit of steam and enjoy
> yourself.

NB: What about the weather?
Mum: Well, it's not warm but it's fine. What more do
you want? You can put an extra coat on or a jumper.
NB: You wouldn't want to go to Spain, where they have
real weather?
Mum: No. They're all foreigners. It's all geared up for
holidays there and for people to go out and be noisy and
rowdy and such like, and we like to go out and do our own
little thing without being sort of cajoled into going out to
the pubs at night and getting drunk. We'd rather be sitting
quietly in the bar at the hotel.

The holiday, for the Billingtons, is viewed as a longer version
of the weekend, a chance for the whole family to be together.
(For younger people, of course, holidays are all about getting
away from family.) Special concessions are made to the children.
They are less subject to discipline. Expenditure is less tightly
controlled. 'Go on. You're on holiday' becomes a standard
excuse for all sorts of small indulgences. The Billingtons have
returned to Great Yarmouth a number of times. Indeed, most of
the guests at their boarding-house return year after year. The
holiday is, for them, no longer a joker card to be played as and
when they like. It has become part of the cycle of the seasons,
part of cyclical time, so that the holiday itself is part of a
cautiously dosed measure of spontaneity.

The odd, liminal state of the seaside is reflected in many of its
institutions. The focus of interest is the beach, that edge of the
country that is neither wholly land nor permanent water, or the
pier, a bridge built out over the sea and going nowhere. Great
Yarmouth has been at pains to re-create an inside beach at its
pleasure centre. Here, artificial waves in an artificial tropical fug
make the whole business of splashing about in the water seem
more natural. Envious spectators, peering in, confirm that patrons must be having fun. Upstairs is an indoor bowling green
with plastic grass.

121

Once the English have got clear of their regular workday identity, the very first thing they must do is send a postcard. Holiday postcards have become an art form in themselves. The English are notoriously unable to say things like 'I care about you' and have developed all manner of small exchanges that carry this message. Exchanges of drinks, hospitality and postcards constitute our everyday social world. Postcards from the seaside have maintained their own self-conscious form of lavatory humour, based on the extraordinary discovery that women have breasts and men have other appendages. They are preserved from the demands of normal gentility by the fact that the seaside is a place of licence, of kiss-me-quick hats and bawdy demeanour. What we write on the back is largely irrelevant. The message is always 'Wish you were here.'

Another feature is the permanent fun-fair. The fair consists principally of rides calculated to confuse and disorientate, to whirl visitors around until they no longer know which way is up or down. You hear them screaming and roaring with laughter, staggering from one ride to another with loud complaints of their suffering. In between, there are ghost trains and distorting mirrors.

A recurring theme of English culture is disorientation to signify periods without structure. This is at its strongest in 'the party'. Parties remain to be studied as a fully anthropological phenomenon, but some of their features are clear. Many parties, for example, dinner parties, are celebrations of structure, with formal dress, stilted behaviour and rich food. Another class of parties is favoured by the young. These parties involve saturation of all the senses with loud music, sometimes flashing lights or, alternatively, very subdued lighting, copious drink, frenetic dancing and licensed sexual activity with partners who might be inaccessible at other times. Parties of both sorts can be used as markers of time. Birthdays, anniversaries or special events that disrupt normal life may require to be marked in these ways. It is normally assumed that the young will opt for marking by disorderly events; older people, by heavily structured occasions.

We visited one night-spot in the town. Rosy O'Grady's caters for an elderly audience in the early part of the evening. A heavily blue-rinsed clientele gather nightly to drink, watch and join in the cabaret. This consists of members of the audience, who sing 'evergreen' songs to the accompaniment of an electric organ. Some are judged extremely bad, others very good. Volume and length of applause designate a winner at the end of the evening, who receives a small prize and great prestige among his peers. It is a scene of rapturous enjoyment. Competition for a table is extreme, the elderly being prepared to wait for hours to be sure of securing one and going to the same club night after night. Later in the evening, the tables are cleared away and young people are admitted for a discothèque. Segregation between the two events is absolute. Each audience faces the other in blank non-comprehension.

Such scenes are puzzling even to the English. They seem designed to refute common generalizations that the English are reserved and subdued. Of course, this was a northern audience. They opined that a southern audience would never be able to 'have fun' in the same way. Thus the apparent unity of a national identity when seen from the outside – the normal anthropological viewpoint – fragments into a thousand different identities when seen from the inside – the native's normal perspective.

The English seem keen, however, to give themselves national characteristics and a national personality, to think of themselves as a single person. This is an approach in keeping with the individualist notion of identity, but one long discarded by anthropology itself, for the characteristics you accord a people depend on your own expectations concerning behaviour. Thus to the Americans, the English appear quaint and incompetent; to South-east Asians, aggressive and uncouth; and to Africans, self-centred and pathetically lonely. The point is that there is no real truth about the supposed character of a people, since words such as 'aggressive' and 'uncouth', although they seem to have clear meanings, are merely relative terms; they contain an inbuilt comparison and the assumption that people act purely out of temperament, not as the result of following cultural rules.

Beyond the self-evident notion of 'fun', what are holidays really for? Some people have argued that they are explicable in terms of psychological pressure. They take the load off our shoulders for a while and so make it possible for us to bear the stresses and strains of the normal working order. This is seen as explaining the fact that the chief requirement of a holiday is to be distinctively unlike everyday life. It is true that English people often speak of holidays in these terms. People do not just 'want' a holiday, they 'need' one. Yet such a view scarcely does justice to the extreme convergence in our culture's idea of what makes a holiday.

As has been suggested, holidays tie up with the ritual of the seasons and notions of time. As the English become wealthier, their holidays simply become more extreme forms of the same thing. Instead of going to Great Yarmouth, we go to Thailand. Instead of distorting mirrors of the fairground, we have the exotic cabaret of the tourist hotel foyer, peoples in whose colourful cultures we may see a refracted image of ourselves. Instead of the self-indulgence of fish and chips on the promenade, we have the beach barbecue. Kiss-me-quick gives way to the free-fire zones of tourist sex.

In the course of making *Native Land* we visited a number of groups who withdraw from mainstream English culture for shorter or longer periods and so are able to maintain a world view quite unlike that of the rest of us. Groups are often able to create their own sense of reality and normality, so that it is those *outside* who look odd. A world view looks normal, indeed inevitable, when you are in it. It is the function of holidays, which are inherently temporary and could never be mistaken for a permanent reality, to make our everyday world seem solid and prevent our seeing it as the tangled web of symbols and conventional presuppositions that we know it to be.

Time is on Our Side

The lunch-break is a treasured moment of freedom within the working day. People spend this precious resource in different ways. Some rush off to do shopping or cope with the mundane chores that have to be done. At the Aetherius Society in London they flee from offices, shops and classrooms to gather in prayer. But like many proselytizing groups outside the mainstream of English culture, the society has a distinctive attitude towards time, an inbuilt concentration on the future.

The Aetherius Society was founded in 1955 and is a body dedicated to the belief that the future of the world will be dominated by a vast extraterrestrial intelligence, which will lead us to a new age of harmony and transformed forms of consciousness. Messages, it is claimed, are received by the group's founder and leader, Sir George King, who hears them in trance from various extraterrestrials and communicates them to his followers.

The reported presence of flying saucers in our skies derives from these extraterrestrial contacts. A perspex model of a flying saucer is on display in the society's office. A neon version flashes above the front door of the premises. One of the society's organizers, the Reverend Steve Gibson, explains the model to us.

Steve: This is actually a model of a certain type of specialized spacecraft, the details of which have been given to us through Sir George . . . Its real size will cover about a mile and a half in length . . . This craft does actually come into orbit of Earth several times of the year for quite a long time. It's normally undetected in radar by design . . . It has a large dome in the top here and through this dome it takes in the sun's rays. That energy then goes down through

125

these pyramid-type crystal structures where it is . . . broken
down . . . The energy is broken down and taken over into
this other ovoid-type crystal and is then slowed down and it
is then sent out through the matrix in the bottom . . . It is
beamed down to Earth whenever it is needed.

The lunch-time prayer sessions of members are part of the
same thing. There is a belief in various sorts of energies, one of
which is prayer-power. When we visited the society, about
twenty members were praying with great fervour. The idea was
that their prayers would be stored in a special battery, which
could then be used for healing or effecting good around the
world. The actual god they might be praying to was seen as
largely irrelevant. It was the power of prayer that was important.
Members snatch a couple of hours from normal work and pay
them into the meter so they can be used for the benefit of
mankind. Further inputs of energy will come from flying saucers.
The efficacy of prayer is held to be almost without limits. Steve explained.

Steve: When the Chernobyl accident took place, we had
prior knowledge . . . about four hours beforehand . . . Sir
George had prior knowledge and we actually did take action.
We have equipment which is capable of radiating energy.
This equipment can radiate power of a spiritual nature . . .
to a particular affected area. We actually ran this equipment
very, very intensively over the course of the weekend. The
incident occurred on a Friday, the Saturday and Sunday no
news got out. It wasn't until the Monday that the tell-tale
signs were picked up in Scandinavia and the word reached
the world's press. Now by that time we'd . . . actually done
our job and finished and packed up, and it was not until
after we'd finished that the word got out.
NB: But the disaster still happened.
Steve: We couldn't weaken it or prevent it. But what we

could do was to help in the aftermath, and maybe, who knows?, people may not be seriously hurt.

It is often the mark of special groups to have less concern with the present than with the future. They have a different relationship with time, for it is the solid-seeming present that is insubstantial. Unlike most of us, Aetherians have a firm notion of what is to be.

Steve: Going back to the great religious writings of the past, many of them have predicted a time of increased turbulence, a quickening of life, followed by a period of drastically improved conditions on Earth. We certainly believe that we are going through this period of turbulence . . . We do believe that eventually world conditions will stabilize and that there will be an era of much greater harmony and enlightenment . . . We do believe that the world's so-called great avatars, the greatest of the great religious leaders of the past, many of them have actually been extraterrestrial. We certainly believe that about Jesus. His origin was from the planet Venus. In the future it won't be done in such a back-door method, as having to incarnate incognito, there will be much more open visitation.

Such beliefs are clearly irregular by our own culture's standards.

NB: Does it worry you that many people would think you were frankly round the bend?
Steve: Well, I think if you hold beliefs such as we hold, then you have to accept that people are going to think you are round the bend. But, by the same token, they thought the man who invented the electric light bulb was round the bend. He was right.
NB: Yes, but to be fair again, throughout history there have been thousands of cases of people who have been

considered round the bend who really were round the bend.
Steve: Absolutely true.

Is such belief in extraterrestrials any more unreasonable than the Christian belief in the Trinity? As *beliefs*, the two seem to have the same status. The principal problem of Aetherianism is one of language, in that it uses the idiom of science (for example, 'prayer-energy') in an unscientific manner. The extraordinary thing about Aetherians is that when not explaining their beliefs, they seem so unremarkable. They are able to dip in and out of the conventional world view, rather as a physicist moves between the worlds of theoretical physics and the world of common-sense knowledge. They are not competing views and segregating them does not involve segregation of self.

A People Apart

We all withdraw occasionally from the everyday world, even if only on holiday. However, there are groups who attempt to create their own everyday world around them and, again, time enters into this. Such a group are the Jehovah's Witnesses.

We visited the Eyre family in Peterborough. Philip and Pauline Eyre are in their early forties and have three teenage children. Jehovah's Witnesses believe in the literal truth of every word of the Bible. They doggedly refuse to think of the Bible as would a historian, literary critic or anthropologist – as a book with a history that is the result of many processes of translation, interpretation, abridgement and rewriting. When we read such a book, inevitably if unconsciously, we subject it to similar processes ourselves in order to 'make sense' of it. Numerous intellectual pratfalls have taught anthropology that what is 'in the text' of any book is far from a simple matter and varies from time to time and place to place. For Witnesses, however, close study of the Bible is not just a guide to conduct that we *may* be able to make relevant to our lives; it is unthinkable that the answer to any problem could lie *outside* the Bible or that the answer given could be ambiguous.

If you can live by one book, life can be very simple, as many academics have found. The certainty that comes from constant deferral to a single text is attractive in itself.

NB: What particularly appealed to you about what they [Jehovah's Witnesses] were saying?
Philip Eyre: I think answers to questions that I'd long had . . . I, at night, sometimes used to wake up and think, 'What's beyond death?' and things like that.
NB: So Jehovah's Witnesses gave you the answers to that?
Philip: Supplied the answers, yes, but not just answers. I think there's one thing that appeals about . . . the Bible itself. It's that it does make sense and when I started to look at it, I was an argumentative soul . . . and it appealed, the logic appealed, so the answers were satisfying.

Jehovah's Witnesses are 'no part of the world' (John 17:16; 15:19), a people apart. They should not involve themselves in the secular empires of the Earth. So while they pay their taxes and keep the law, they do not vote or adopt ritual attitudes to such things as the flag or the royal family.

Philip: We . . . obviously wouldn't view things in quite the same way as somebody who looks upon themselves as a really fine upstanding Briton . . . The royal family, as a figurehead, if you like, of the country in which we live, we have respect for them. My wife is always interested in the movements of them, especially births of babies and so on. In

that sense, you know, it's family, isn't it? So in that sense, although maybe we wouldn't view the flag and the royal family in quite the same way, we do have a great respect.
NB: But more the sort of respect of an outsider rather than an enthusiastic participant?
Philip: If you want to put it that way, yes.

Witnesses tend to keep to themselves, except, of course, during their proselytizing activities. A strong sense of community is immediately evident.

NB: And as a Jehovah's Witness, you are obviously a member of a special group. Does it have strong sense of community?
Philip: Yes, yes. The congregations do. First and foremost the congregation that we are associated with now . . . is brought together to get the work done. But, naturally, we have fine, close friends within the congregation and enjoy each other's company very much indeed.
NB: And do you find that most of your friends tend to be Witnesses?
Philip: I would have to say yes to that. It seems to be a natural thing. I think that's true in perhaps a lot of societies, isn't it? You're drawn to those that you have a great deal in common with.

In fact, Witnesses are wary of contact with outsiders except in their missionary role. The parameters for contact with outsiders having been set in such a confrontational fashion, missionary work clearly distinguishes Witnesses and makes them proclaim that separate identity in public. Although Philip is a television engineer, he maintains rigorous control over what programmes are watched in his home, lest the outside creep in and erode the family's own world view.

Philip: If you are continually watching programmes that
are not suitable, then it becomes acceptable to you. You're
starting to come and share the standards, if you like, of the
people that you are associating with . . . We don't view it
that 'when in Rome . . .' We prefer not to do what the
Romans do.

So Witnesses tend not to join clubs or play games with
outsiders, marry them or spend spare time with them. Much
time is spent together in close study of the Bible. These sessions
may last for hours and Witnesses always have a Bible to hand.
Even children attend and show (for England) astonishing self-
control and dedication. Through these marathons of like-minded
discussion, where everyone uses the same techniques on the
same text to come to the same conclusion, they come to see the
world *as* Witnesses. It is hard to imagine how else they could
maintain a wall against the values of the culture that has them
surrounded. There are other presentations where Witnesses are
advised on technique and how to argue their case forcefully or
use different arguments according to the age and interests of
other parties. Witnesses learn from childhood to state cogently
who they are and what they believe in a way that seems at
variance with the English norms of what should be stated and
what merely implied. Philip regards as very British the notion of
religion as a private thing not to be discussed.

Philip: In England . . . I don't know . . . British reserve
maybe . . . people say, 'I don't discuss religion.' . . . It's
perhaps due to the fact that privacy is considered a very big
thing in England.

This is most marked when Jehovah's Witnesses appear on our
doorsteps and try to convert us.

Philip: I think it's well for people to understand the inner feelings that have to be overcome by Jehovah's Witnesses who have that inborn Englishness. It's difficult for us to generate the energy necessary sometimes to go from door to door . . . We certainly do not find it easy. In fact, sometimes, it's extremely hard.

NB: Can I be a little insidious now and suggest that Jehovah's Witnesses were born as a movement in America? Do you think it would be less difficult to go out and evangelize in an American context?

Philip: I suppose that's possible . . . I find there's a greater openness with Americans.

The Jehovah's Witnesses also have different notions of time and a different chart of the future. They do not celebrate birthdays or Christmas or Easter. Moreover, the linchpin of their identity is that the end of the world as we know it is nigh. We are running out of time.

Like everything else, this idea derives from biblical sources, especially Revelations, one of the more ecstatic books, regarded with some distaste by many Church of England clerics. The message of the prophecies for Witnesses is that the final phase of this present world began in 1914 and is to be a time of chaos. During the lifetime of the generation born then, Armageddon, the annihilation of the ungodly and the establishment of God's Kingdom on Earth will all come to pass. It could happen any day now and Jehovah's Witnesses have it in writing.

NB: Do you live in constant anticipation of that day coming?

Philip: Yes, yes. We keep awake . . . and we try to view the days as urgent and, of course, spend as much time as we can preaching to other people.

NB: Does that mean that you regard the whole of your present life as a very provisional, purely temporary thing?

Philip: I suppose we, in a sense, do look upon ourselves as alien residents, a bit like Abraham did, you know, when he had to up stakes and move out of the land where he was born.

NB: Is that part of your being apart from the world? Really there's no need to concern yourself with it because it's only going to last for a few years anyway?

Philip: Yes. The scriptures speak about the *real* life, getting hold of the real life, as a matter of interest. So we look upon our lives now – we enjoy life, it's not all preaching as you perhaps have already gathered – so we look upon our *existence* as quite permanent really. We've grown used to the idea, if you like, of not looking upon life as temporary, but rather everlasting.

NB: But you would therefore tend to live rather more in the future than in the present?

Philip: I don't know. That's a difficult one to answer in a sense. I suppose we're just getting used to living for ever.

Green Time

Most of the methods for measuring the lapse of time have, I believe, been the contrivance of monks and religious recluses, who, finding time hang heavy on their hands, were at some pains to see how they got rid of it.*

Old Hall, Bergholt, East Anglia, used to house a community of Franciscan monks. Now the altar has been removed and the chapel is converted to a theatre. Since 1975 it has been the home of Old Hall Community, a group of some eighty like-minded people who have come here to farm about sixty acres of

*William Hazlitt, 'On a Sundial', *Sketches and Essays*, 1839

the countryside communally and in accordance with 'organic' philosophy. They try to grow their own food, treat their animals humanely and promote, by example rather than preaching, the proposition that the world cannot sustain the consumer life-style and that a simpler alternative is both necessary and desirable. Mike Baker, a founding member, explains:

> *Mike:* I suppose we were anxious about the higher
> technological society, the way society was moving in
> consumerism, in not caring for the land. It was born very
> much of the Seventies feeling towards self-sufficiency . . .
> but we realized nevertheless that in doing that we couldn't
> be totally self-sufficient. One thing that went very much in
> our favour, because the Franciscan friars were very much
> liked locally . . . they listened to us when we wanted to live
> here and they believed in us and I shall never forget their
> remarks officially about us when they said, 'Well, here is
> obviously a group who, although they haven't a religious
> bond which is overtly obvious, nevertheless for other, but
> similar, reasons want to live in a fashion like we lived here
> and we feel very happy for them.'

It was in monasteries that clocks and Western notions of time were invented, the day being carved up into different zones, each of which had its attendant duties. But time always has at least two aspects that can be stressed, the linear and the circular. Ecological thought is pervasively concerned with cycles rather than simple relations of immediate cause and effect. Each mode of thought becomes loaded with different moral values. Simple cause-and-effect linear relations are associated with exploitative thinking and are bad. Cyclical thinking is ecologically sound and good in itself.

The bell above the chapel now summons not to prayer but to communal meals, which have replaced prayer as the principal ritual marker of the day, the unity of the group and the dependence of all on the land. Most necessary tasks are assigned by a cyclical rota, which is also a device against permanent hierarchy. John Gamlin, another founder member:

> *John:* I think the rota represents, for many people, that which is central . . . namely, that we should eat together, as a communal activity . . .
> *NB:* Why is that so important?
> *John:* Well, I suppose it's a bit of ritual really and eating together – as I think right through our history – has been seen as a place where a family comes together, where in religious circles . . . where a Church comes together to the communion table and here, where the community comes together. There's no other place that we come together other than in meetings, so I see it as ritualistic as much as practical.

The group see themselves very much as planting their own life-style back in the English countryside. Organic metaphors abound. Indeed, members stress that the community is not merely the embodiment of principles, it has grown and changed 'organically', the same argument used in mainstream English culture to defend the apparent irrationality of institutions such as the monarchy. In Old Hall Community, given the emphasis on harmony, making difficult decisions is necessarily fraught with awkwardness, since no display of disagreement or naked power is in keeping with the community's values.

> *Mike:* The decisions can be a lengthy and painful process . . . It can be very demanding. It is done largely by consensus decision.

The group expresses its communal identity through communal possessions, the house and land, but this extends down to the minor articles of the household.

135

Mike: Living in a community does give ways of co-operating which reduce consumerism, of sharing washing, sharing the products we buy, buying with the commercial implications of what you are buying in mind, buying things which are ecologically sound.

Yet the Community is only too aware of its own problem of inbuilt exclusiveness. Because of the inflation of property values, to buy into the joint property of the commune – the house and land – requires a large amount of cash, anywhere from £8,000 to £42,000.

Mike: Anything that creates a separatism, an élitism, I think we've tried to avoid, although you could arguably say that we are middle-class, English, white people living here in a rural setting. This is where a lot gets thrown at us.

Unlike the Jehovah's Witnesses, the Community encourages visitors of different views, hangs on to links with 'surrounding villagers' and erects no wall of exclusiveness, yet economic pressures and the urge to self-sufficiency conspire to cut it off from all but those like themselves.

Mike: My beliefs reflect what 'us – we as a group' do. They've changed as we've realized that we could easily be cutting ourselves off from society by being self-sufficient, by being nomadic and knitting our own woolly hats from our sheep's wool, etc.

A simple opposition structures the relations between the myth of modernization and the myth of the countryside. To community members, the Smallwood model of farming, with its machines and chemicals – so 'natural' to us – is the worst sort of over-technical exploitation of the environment. Technology is regarded with deep suspicion, while the countryside is naturally good. The ecological mode of thinking, moreover, leads to the equation of 'natural' ways of farming and social organization.

Mike: To live in a rural surrounding and to be able to work on the land, being in touch with the seasons and the phases of the moon, puts one back in touch with oneself, and for many people who are lost in their urban living life-style . . . they're out of touch with that. And that is sad.

John Gamlin echoes the same view:

John: I would like to think that to some extent we all come back into contact with the soil. It seems to me a lot of people lead a very artificial life, living in tiny little houses, with a pocket handkerchief of a back garden, and are thoroughly dependent upon the shop and outside suppliers. Technology at one time was making the world a better place but it's too much of it and it's generating its own problems of one kind or another, like conflict, like vandalism, like divorce. These are symptoms of the social malaise which have come about because of the kind of life-style that we live.

The rejection of the technological roller-coaster, the stressing of natural rhythms of organic growth – these amount to a sort of 'green time' that is unconcerned with clock time, the mark of wage labour and the outside world. It has often been remarked that innovations such as cameras, railways, radio and television have transformed the way we see space and time, but it is seldom noted that attitudes towards such technology can literally put the clock back. The fact that Community members navigate in time by the Community bell and scarcely bother with clocks shows their divorce from linear time. 'Green time' is inherently circular, like the rota that organizes work allocations. The key word for the Community is 'harmony', a term that normally implies the metaphoric mapping of features from one area of

137

thought to another. Thus harmony with natural rhythms will inevitably heal divisions in the human world.

> *John:* The object of the community is to unite people, and unite Man and his environment. I think what we're concerned about these days is divisions within society, so we're concerned about the healing of divisions and also to generate harmony. I suppose that's what we're concerned about in the wider setting: that we all relate one to another, all of creation, and yet there seems to be antagonism. There's conflict and I think we see ourselves as trying to bring harmony.

But time has another aspect – the past – and it is to this that we must turn to see identity given national form through the monarchy.

6 Queen and Country

*A French bastard landing with an armed banditti and
establishing himself King of England, against the consent
of the natives, is, in plain terms, a very paltry, rascally
original. It certainly hath no divinity in it . . . The plain
truth is that the antiquity of English monarchy will not
bear looking into.*

Tom Paine, *Common Sense*, 1776

THERE IS LITTLE doubt that the institution of royalty is nowadays extremely popular in England, even if such was not always the case. Yet when it comes to the game of national identity, the royal family are something of an over-used trump card. They turn up everywhere, heading regiments, charities, youth organizations, even religions. Their presence on the governing boards of such institutions marks each of these as 'a good thing'; their absence is grounds for suspicion. Such is the mark of persons who have ceased to be individuals and become symbols.

It is one of the inconveniences of living symbols that they talk and act. A great part of the popular press and the English national consciousness concerns itself with tedious discussions of whether what the human members of the royal family actually say and do is compatible with their symbolic role. It is probably significant that this is perceived by the English in terms of 'public' and 'private', that is, as a matter of the right of the prominent individual to enjoy privacy.

The Queen is Queen of England, yet her domain has been stretched to include all the British and, indeed, the rump of the Commonwealth. She is a curious being. When she crosses the Scottish border, she automatically changes her religion in keeping with local notions. She has two birthdays. English usage makes fine distinctions between the Queen, the Crown and the Government, but there is a sense in which all are corporate entities. It is not clear whether legally she still has two bodies, as in the Middle Ages.

As the previous sentence shows, it is impossible to write of the Queen without doing violence to time. Her curious relationship with time is hinted at in her mystical ability to define states of existence. She declares laws valid, makes the humble noble, the convicted innocent, moves an entire nation from one symbolic state to another in the declaration of war and – at a humbler but more time-consuming level – declares bridges and other public works open. Usually, this involves specially closing them for the day. Her legitimacy centres upon the possession of ancient heir-looms, the Crown Jewels.

In the study of symbolism two crude types of symbol can be distinguished: the 'lumpers' and the 'splitters'. The latter are used in ways that mark fine but important distinctions. Thus everyday material possessions can be used to make infinitely fine discriminations between those that own them. British royalty, on the other hand, is the ultimate 'lumper', a unifying and rallying mark that attempts to surmount divisions of race, creed, class and even period, that incorporates and fuses other powerful symbolic, semantic and emotional elements into a single heady brew. Important constituents are fidelity, legitimacy, hierarchy; but they are not the most important. Royalty is, above all, the mark of the complex and continuing British national identity. 'The King is dead! Long live the King!' eloquently expresses the fact that royalty embodies an immunity to change.

The unwritten British constitution acknowledges this in the opposition between politics and royalty. Politics is the epitome of inconstant fortune, reversal and provisionality. Royalty stands above and apart from this, the enduring source of the legitimacy of governments.

The Over-used Trump

English people swear loyalty to the Queen in all sorts of situations. Many start about the age of eight when they join the Wolf Cubs or Brownies or, later in life, the Scouts and Guides. All these are organizations that try to subsume the individual in some sort of group identity, usually seen as a *higher* identity.

Institutions of applied dottiness, such as the Guides, are woven into the very fabric of English life. It is curious that they have been a major export success since they embody very English ideas about the natural goodness of the countryside, God and the monarch. They are implicitly patriotic. (The Queen and Queen Mother are patrons of the Guides, Princess Margaret is president). Indeed, the explicit purpose of the founding of Guiding was to find a role for women in building up the Empire. But how deep does this patriotism go? We visited a troop of Guides in camp at Clitheroe.

It was a cold, damp day and there was a desperate determination to be busy. As they hauled water, emptied lavatory buckets and practised building rafts, the Guides maintained, with something akin to defiance, that they *were* enjoying themselves. The ever-slippery word 'fun' was invoked.

The Guides are an early example of applied anthropology, embodying one man's vision of the native peoples of South Africa fused with the traditions of the British Army. Thus there are various 'colours' ceremonies involving the Union Jack and other flags. Community singing and uniforms are ways of building group identity that are borrowed from the armed forces. Camp is a special place with all manner of arcane traditions that mark it off from normality. Unlike American Guides, the British do not transfer ash from their last camp fire to their present location to express the common identity of campsites. They do, however, take camp names (nicknames). These can stick for life. We spoke to Ivy 'Squidge' Coles – a retired lady still so named because some forty years before she trod in a particularly nasty cowpat – about the Guide Promise:

> *I promise that I will do my best*
> *To do my duty to God*
> *To serve the Queen and help other people and*
> *To keep the Guide Law.*

Squidge: We do have a religious centre to our guiding, so we do include God in our, sort of, everyday Guiding life.

143

It's part of our Promise. We promise to do our duty to God.
NB: What does that mean exactly?
Squidge: Ah. This is something that we ask girls when
they're about to become Guides – what they think it is. I
wonder whether it would help if you asked a Guide.

So we did.

NB: In the Promise, the Guide's Promise, you promise to
serve the Queen. Is that important to you?
Emma Bruce: Sometimes. You think more at camp than
when you're at home.
NB: Do you find that all the little ceremonies are
important for that? The 'colours' and such like?
Emma: Yes.
NB: They do make you think about it?
Emma: Yes . . . Sometimes we have colours, the company
does, when we're at home, but it's completely different
because you're inside and not outside.
NB: And what about serving God? That's part of the
Promise too, isn't it?
Emma: Yes.
NB: Is that important to you? Do you really believe in
that?
Emma: No, I don't believe in God but I do believe in
prayers.
NB: You'll have to explain that to me . . .
Emma: I don't know. I've just got used to it because at
the end of every day at camp, we always have prayers and
I've just got used to it, but I don't believe in them.

We tried another.

NB: As a guide, you make the Promise. Is it taken very
seriously?

Sarah Curtis: Yes.

NB: To serve the Queen. You promise to serve the Queen . . . What does . . .?

Sarah: Helping other people, being friendly, trusting and all that.

NB: Is that serving the Queen?

Sarah: Sort of.

NB: But what does it mean to you to serve the Queen?

Sarah: To keep the Guide Law.

NB: And all that's part of serving the Queen . . .

Sarah: Yes, it's respecting Lord Baden-Powell and Lady Baden-Powell.

We went back to Squidge for a definition of 'serving the Queen'.

Squidge: To be good citizens. Just to keep the law. I think this is very important . . .

NB: So that 'the Queen' is not just *personally* serving the Queen . . .

Squidge: No. It's serving the country, that's it.

It looks as if the notion of 'serving the Queen' has become absorbed in that of being a good citizen, a rather different thing. It seems, indeed, somewhat difficult to imagine a Guide caught in the act of 'not serving the Queen'. It could only be one of those catch-all offences, such as 'unAmerican activities' or 'action likely to bring the university into disrepute', that they use when they can't get you for anything else.

Soldiers of the Queen

When Scouts and Guides grow up, they may well find theselves obliged to renew their oath of allegiance in the armed forces, whose duty is formally to the Queen. We visited the King's Own Border Regiment of the Territorial Army in Barrow-in-Furness to see how far these soldiers held themselves to be 'soldiers of the Queen' and how important this was for group identity.

Although it was a weekday, they were on exercises, capturing an abandoned barn occupied by an enemy agent. Most of the men were on strike from the Vickers shipyards. Their officer, Alan Dickson, worked in the administration of the same company and was therefore *not* on strike. When Territorial Army men put on the Queen's uniform, they become subject to a different law (an officer is subject to Queen's Regulations all the time). Was there not a problem switching between the two identities, especially during an industrial dispute?

Alan: I would never let anything like that rub off on the
T A and neither would the lads. If there was anyone who
tried that, I would stamp on it very hard and I would expect
the N C Os to do that as well because the T A is something
totally different. It's a totally different set-up. It's a disciplined
organization. They cannot go around insulting people as they
might do in a strike situation.
NB: So they could shout at you on a picket line but they
call you 'sir' down at the T A?
Alan: Oh yes . . .
NB: And people can compartmentalize their lives to that
degree?

Alan: They have to learn to. It's the only way it's going
to work.

When you talk to the men themselves, it's clear that it *does*
work. To be asked to play the enemy on exercises is a form of
punishment. There is a quite fierce group spirit in the platoon
and it is this that is the main attraction for the men and the
reason most joined up.

NB: What were you looking for when you joined up?
Graham Seaward: See some mates, really. Get some friends.
NB: You didn't feel you had any?
Graham: Well, yes. But there's a bit more in it. It's just
all together. It's mucking in, you know, working as a team.
It's getting down and doing it.
NB: And you don't get that in civilian life?
Graham: No, not in Vickers you don't. If you get a job,
you do it on your own and that's it.

John Rawlinson, another platoon member, was similarly attrac-
ted by comradeship.

John: T A is a separate life. I have separate friends outside
and I have friends in the T A. I think some of the extremes
we suffer together going out on night exercises, getting
frozen, being taken to the limit of your sort of physical
endurance, I think that makes us special sort of friends.
NB: People who have done studies of these things say that
in the regular army, in battle situations, it's not the 300 years
of regimental tradition that count, it's those local loyalties to
your mates, to your comrades. Do you think that's true?
John: Yes, I would say that's very true. I know even
when we're training out and we're training with blanks . . .
in a situation where it's not life and death, but we get the
feeling if another company's going to take one of our fellows

prisoner or anything, the loyalty's there. We've worked together, we've trained together, suffered together and there's a lot of loyalty, a lot of loyalty.

The uniform is part of this. It imposes identity upon its wearers but denies individual variation or caprice, rendering dress deliberately inexpressive of personality in contrast to normal life. Upon this is then imposed a series of minor differences, each of which can be assigned a definite meaning, rank, affiliation, special skills and so on. Such matters of identity and hierarchy are only subtly and ambiguously expressed in civilian life. In military dress they are wholly explicit and can be easily translated into power. It is clear from dress who has the right to give orders to whom, unlike in civilian life. Alan Dickson was perfectly conscious of its personal importance to him.

Alan: Uniform is important in that it brings everyone at once down to the one level. You all look the same with minor variations and then you've got the badges of rank on the uniforms, which distinguish some people from the mass of the private soldiers, either on the arms for the NCOs or on the shoulders for the officers, but you've still got the green uniform on and you're still a soldier whatever rank you are.
NB: And you actually *feel* a difference when you put that uniform on?
Alan: Yes.
NB: You switch from one identity to the other?
Alan: Yes, I do. Very easily.

What then of the Queen? A number of members of the platoon remarked that they had never held themselves to be particularly patriotic but that being in the Territorials had made them more so.

NB: Can you tell us what your oath of allegiance was?
Simon Gray: We swear to protect the Queen and country

148

and anyone we're called on. Basically, we're there to be
called on when the country needs us.

NB: Does that mean you're all a bunch of arch-patriots?

Simon: I don't think we are when we join, but I think
the TA makes you patriotic, yes. I think I'm more patriotic
since I joined, yes . . .

NB: But your actual oath of loyalty is to the Queen. Is
the Queen very important to you personally?

Simon: No, I wouldn't say so . . . Not the Queen herself.
Yes, there's a sense of loyalty there to the Queen as a
figurehead, but as much to the company as anything.

Alan Dickson, the company commander, agreed.

Alan: [The average TA man] probably hasn't thought
much about Queen and country before he joins. He's
probably in favour of the monarchy, fairly sure about that
. . . When he gets into the TA, there's a sort of ambience in
the TA that starts to rub off on a man and does to a greater
extent the longer he stays in the TA . . . When it gets down
to it in the field, your loyalty is to your section and to your
mates around you. I don't think anyone would dispute that,
but you *are* fighting for Queen and country . . . You stick
together and you look after your own against outsiders.

NB: Is that something you think people miss from normal
work?

Alan: Yes. I don't particularly think that there's much
loyalty to your employer . . .

So here, loyalty to Queen and country need not necessarily
involve a soldier's feelings in a very active way. The Queen is
seen not as a real human symbol that embodies all sorts of
abstract values; she seems to be seen as abstract and shadowy. A
soldier carries out his obligations towards such abstract beings
just by doing his duty, rather as the Guides do by being good

149

citizens. The loyalty of the TA to the Queen is seen as a more general expression of the fierce loyalty to comrades.

Yet perhaps there is more to talking about loyalty than mere feelings. Every culture has rules about the things that may and may not be said explicitly in words. The English are notoriously disinclined to express their deepest feelings in language, reluctant to strike high moral attitudes. It is interesting that sociological explanation will easily accept the reduction of high principle to individual utilitarianism (mean, self-serving strategy), but not vice versa. This is now part of our model of a universal human nature and makes us unwilling to accept expressions of loyalty to a grouping higher than ourselves unless we can find that it conceals some more selfish end.

> *NB:* People nowadays tend to be very cynical about
> concepts like loyalty and patriotism. Do you think that
> beneath that cynicism there are, perhaps, deep wells of these
> qualities waiting to be tapped in all of us?
> *Alan:* Yes, I think there are. I can be perfectly cynical
> about it myself, but I am a patriot and I think that the
> reaction of the majority of the population in 1982 [the
> Falklands War] showed that those things did exist and it
> just needed something to trigger it off.

A Sense of History

If you ask about national identity, one word keeps recurring: history. It is assumed that the reality of national identity is *proved* by history. In fact, of course, it only makes things much more problematic, for history is constructed from the viewpoint of the present, which is why it is always changing. Indeed, we impose on the past our present notion of national identity. English people will thus confidently inform foreigners that 'we' were conquered by the Romans – before England as an entity even existed.

The very borders of history are arbitrarily fixed. Officially, history begins thirty years ago, with the thirty-years rule that makes public records accessible. This is about the same limit that school history and even academic history assign. As we grow older, we increasingly come into conflict with the historical perspective. It is applied to periods that we feel more properly to belong to our own biographies. It is not history, we may protest, it is our own remembered past.

History is, above all, a source that we can mine for myths. The past becomes a proof of essential 'Englishness'. Each nation constructs a history of itself like those different maps where the nationality of a cartographer is clear from the nation he puts in the middle of the world. This is perhaps clearest in our money. Nothing seems more real than money, yet it is merely a metaphor that expresses the value of goods in terms of an arbitrary standard. The relatively valueless pieces of paper that we hoard and exchange are encrusted with national symbols. Female symbols such as Boadicea (who would not have understood what 'English' meant) and Britannia (allegedly modelled on a royal mistress) jostle St George (who apparently never existed but is a popular figure in voodoo cults) – all as marks of that 'Englishness'. On the other side of the notes, we have the national poet (Shakespeare) or national heroes, Wellington (destroying some French) and Florence Nightingale (engaged in feminine ministrations to the wounded). On all denominations we have the head of the Queen in state dress. It is her head that transforms these pieces of paper into national currency. The monarchy, the history, the wealth – all confirm and reinforce each other.

Nowadays we take our symbols very seriously. 'Our' history is not just a time, it is a place and we expect to be able to go there as we might go to Torremolinos. It is housed in the bricks and mortar – or, more usually, stone and mortar – of national monuments, which are preserved in timelessness. When time attacks them, they are painstakingly 'restored'. When we do not have enough, we build some more. The creation of historical 'theme parks' is a major growth industry. They peddle a sanitized form of history, picturesque rather than discomforting, unifying rather than divisive, where exploitative labour is absorbed into rustic craft. They bear the same relation to academic history that tourism does to ethnography.

Nowadays, many special sites exist – waxwork museums and *son et lumière* shows – that cater specifically for tourists. They pose an easy answer to the question of who the English (or British, or Scots) *are* and where their historical essence is to be found. The picture postcards that the tourists send home offer us a caricature of ourselves-as-others-see-us in the endless photographs of royalty, military uniforms and castles. But it should not be thought that such things exist just for gullible foreigners. We, too, are gluttonous consumers of our own historical myths.

The Stately Homes of England

> *The stately homes of England, how beautiful they stand,*
> *To prove the upper classes have still the upper hand . . .*
> *The stately homes of England, we proudly represent,*
> *We only keep them up for Americans to rent.*
>
> Noel Coward

The aristocracy are viewed as having some sort of monopoly on family history and are mysteriously described as coming from 'old' families. Hutton-in-the-Forest, Cumbria, is the family seat of Lord Inglewood. It has been in the family since the seventeenth century and stands on a working estate of some 10,000 acres.

The house is a mixture of styles, having evolved over many hundreds of years, but is unlike many stately homes in that it is still very much lived in as a family home. It thus combines, for visitors, those two major great obsessions of the English: the home and history.

The Honourable Richard Vane, heir to the title, is a young man who is very concerned with the English identity, being a candidate for the European Parliament as well as a member of an ancient house. We asked him his views on the place of history in our national identity.

Richard: I think that whatever is seen as being British identity does evolve over time. I am a pro-European. I am not an out-and-out federalist or anything like that, but I think you've got to see your own identity in the context of what is happening in the world around. It's interesting, if you go back to the Middle Ages, Britain, Ireland and, perhaps taking Britain as a whole, England and Scotland were very much part of Europe. I think you can very strongly argue that the whole of our colonial history was really fighting European wars outside Europe. After all, we very rarely fought the indigenous population of what became colonies. It was normally the French or the Spaniards and it was all to do with power politics back in Europe . . .

NB: And do you think the aristocracy still have a role to play in maintaining our national identity?

Richard: It's very difficult to answer, I think, because you've identified a group that doesn't really exist any more. If, for example, you're a member of the aristocracy and you have a place like this, there is clearly, I think, an identifiable role in the maintenance aspect of Britain's cultural history. If you happen to be, just to quote a mythical example, a down-and-out duke quietly drinking himself to death in Pinner, I'm not quite sure what role you do have.

NB: Where would the Queen fit into all this? One of the

153

anomalies, I suppose, about the Queen is that although she is a member of the aristocracy, she is somehow perceived as a very middle-class figure.

Richard: Yes. I think the monarchy has been very clever at adapting itself to the world we are now living in, because, quite regardless of whether any particular person is a republican or a monarchist or something somewhere in the middle, you've got to accept that the majority of the British people love the monarchy . . . It's very difficult, I think, to logically argue the case of the monarchy once you accept that the Divine Right of Kings argument is nonsense – which I think is a completely unsustainable approach – yet we have, it appears, a system which gives satisfaction to most of the people, and in a democratic society, a free society, people should have what they want. It seems they want the monarchy and so to that extent everybody's happy.

Yet there seems an inherent vagueness about the English identity. Richard Vane sees a historical explanation to all this.

Richard: It may be that we are still culturally living on the inheritance of our Victorian, imperial past when, quite clearly, we British – within that definition, the English – were top dogs. There was no need then, I don't think, to define in an introverted way who you were and what you were doing. And I think we've lived off that for quite a long time. I dare say that as the world moves on, we may find it more important to be clear in our minds about who we are as a nation, because some people are unhappy about nationality and nationalism. But it does, whether you like it or not, play a very strong part in many people's minds and, when all is said and done, the people in this island will band together if the nation is threatened.

In another context Richard alluded to a house of his acquaintance, so overstuffed with objects during the Victorian period that

154

current inhabitants may survive largely by selling them off, which merely reduces the amount of furniture to normal modern standards. It is curious that in the midst of this piling up of objects, our Victorian forebears should not have felt the need to furnish themselves with a clear self-definition.

The Fans

Cool constitutional analyses and antiquarian interest aside, there is a much more enthusiastic and personal brand of royalism abroad in the land, a love not just for monarchy but for the monarch herself. We went to see Elizabeth Barron, a self-confessed royalist fanatic, at her home in Bretherton, near Preston. She lives in a small bungalow distinguished principally by the display of numerous Union Jacks and pictures of the royal family around the doorway. The garden was ornamented with a large anchor executed in empty margarine tubs and a doll hanging from a stork's beak. Elizabeth explained that they were to mark the birth of a child to Prince Andrew.

NB: Why do you like the royal family?
Elizabeth: It's just something I can't explain. It's like falling in love with somebody, but you can't give a reason for it. It's just the same with me and the royal family. I just can't give you a reason.

Elizabeth has spent several holidays near the royal estates and met the Queen several times. She speaks of these meetings as the great events of her life.

Elizabeth: I've spent many holidays at Windsor during Royal Ascot week, and I used to stand at the gate at Old Windsor waiting for the Queen returning . . . She always came in at a private entrance, so one of the estate workers told me which entrance it was and I used to stand as near as I could without breaking the law, and I always waved to her and she always waved back and after a few years, I thought, 'Oh I wonder if she would accept a posy from me.' So I wrote and asked her . . . and I've written twice since then and each time she's accepted one. The cars have stopped there and it's been lovely and she's chatted to me for about five minutes.

Elizabeth's face still lights up at the telling of it.

Elizabeth: She was lovely. I travelled down on the Saturday morning and my hands were all hot and clammy and the Queen's were just like rose petals, they were really.

The other great event was attending Princess Margaret's wedding (Elizabeth has attended four royal weddings and two coronations), at which a pocket was torn off her coat by the *royal* car! Although an elderly widow living with evident signs of economy, Elizabeth worries about accusations that the royal family are a waste of money. She has compiled a dossier of cuttings to support her case that they are a financial asset to the country.

NB: But do you think it's right to think of the royal family in terms of cash?
Elizabeth: No, the royal family can't be assessed in terms of cash at all. They are absolutely priceless and I think they are our greatest national asset.

Every culture develops rules for the control of those two most disruptive idioms of exchange, money and humour. The Queen, for Elizabeth, as a fundamental cultural value, should not be expressed in a balance sheet any more than she should be joked about.

156

Margaret Barron, Elizabeth's sister, takes a somewhat different position.

Margaret: I don't go to the lengths that Elizabeth goes to because I don't feel the need to. I think if everyone did it, it would be a big interference. I don't feel any need to come close. I like them at a distance as well as close.
Elizabeth: It's just unthinkable that we should interfere with all the history and heritage that many, many millions of us are so proud of. It's just unthinkable that we should abolish the monarchy and become a republic. I mean, there's a thrill about the monarchy that there isn't about a republic.

Elizabeth subscribes to a royalist magazine and keeps scrapbooks of letters and photographs relating to her visits to royal events. It is reminiscent of the way people in English culture behave towards film stars. Elizabeth would reject the assimilation of royalty to mere celebrity, but there is no doubt that for many they are on a par. The more scurrilous Sunday newspapers exist almost entirely on explorations of the private lives of soap opera stars and 'royals'. It is clear that nowadays soap operas have become a model by which the English understand the royal family. They have the same glamour, wealth and unreality, and the public expect to read about their scandals hidden behind a flimsy façade.

Approaching the Presence

In our attempt to see the other side of the coin, we were unable to interview the Queen herself. Instead, we visited Jeanette Charles, 'a person who looks very much like Her Majesty'. Jeanette is an actress, who often acts the part of the

Queen at openings and is, indeed, often mistaken for her. She is very much a sign of a symbol. It is rare in anthropology to find second order symbols ready to interpret themselves.

NB: It seems very strange that people should want you to 'deputize' for the Queen – after all you're not the real one.
Jeanette: Yes, I know. It's always seemed rather odd to me, but you see we're in the world now of television. I find it very difficult, of course, to be out and about now amongst the public as much as I used to, but the Queen is so well respected that time and time again people come up to me and say, 'We know you're Jeanette Charles, but it's so much like seeing the Queen, we'd like to tell you this and we'd like to tell you that.' Then they talk about how they feel about the Queen . . . and it's almost as if I'm an agony aunt most of the time. It's almost as if *I'm* secondary. It's a strange thing.
NB: What does the monarchy mean? What do the people think the Queen is for?
Jeanette: The Queen is history. The monarchy is history. The Queen is part of that, of blood and of heritage . . . I can't imagine how it would be to be without [a royal family]. I really can't. We are a very small part of the world. We are respected as Britons. Wherever I go in the world I think British people, there is something about us . . . we have a certain perception. We have a quickness of understanding and we are . . . respected, strangely enough, throughout the world. I say, 'strangely', because with so many movements in the world with ethnic people and so on one would think that perhaps we are not considered terribly British. We still are. The royalty is Britain and Britain is the royalty.

Perhaps so. But the strange things about the British royal family is that they have been able to impose themselves as a sort of meta-royalty, a royalty among royals. All over the world, nations have perfectly acceptable royal families of their own.

Yet they slavishly concern themselves with gossip about the private life of the British royals, known only from newspapers and television. Among royals, they are *stars*.

There is another aspect to our increasing concern with their reality as living people that in no way undermines their effectiveness as symbols.

> *Jeanette:* I'm almost the same age as the Queen. I have manners. I have respect. I have loyalty and love. I *do* expect the royal family to show an example. They are being paid by the public . . . I *do* expect a very moral example from the royal family and I know a lot of people do.

In other words, we expect them to live their private lives according to a morality we may no longer keep ourselves. We expect them to symbolically live our private lives *for* us – to be the public face of private family life.

The British, the English and All the Rest

The English identity seems, at first sight, curiously undersupported by the trappings of nationality. We have a national day that is almost totally ignored. Indeed, few English people know when it is. The national flag is rarely seen and even the Union Jack – after a brief appearance as a fashion accessory in the Sixties – is more likely to be carried by a hooligan than a patriot. We lack national costume or cuisine. In the political sphere we lack a written constitution. We don't even have a national language, just a class accent.

To foreigners, of course, the Scots, Irish and Welsh are all English too. However, within the UK the English identity looks strangely empty; it is all the other identities that are marked. Englishness is simply the identity that all the rest define themselves *against*. Englishness operates at two levels. It is a regional identity, like Scottish, which is why those of Asian or Caribbean descent born in England tend to describe themselves as 'British' rather than 'English'. We are perhaps moving to a stage where it is possible to have more than one ethnic identity – rather as Americans may hold themselves to be *both* American and Greek or Irish. But for the moment Englishness appropriates the symbols of Britishness to itself. So the English Queen is now Queen of all the British and on the way to being some sort of international meta-monarch. English is the mother tongue of Britons and also the language of international modernity. It all has about it the air of arrogance of British postage stamps: because we invented stamps, it is for everyone *else* to identify *theirs*. The Queen's head stares out in unquestioning presumption. Stamps are British unless otherwise defined. Thus it is with Englishness.

Endnotes

My field assistant, Jim Batchelor, is a patriotic man, proud to be English. The royal family is part of that, though he has less concern for what another informant termed 'the Yuppie children, the spare parts lying around waiting for a constitutional breakdown'. A picture of the Queen Mother is tacked up in his van.

NB: You're a bit of a royalist, aren't you?
Jim: I like the royal family, yeah. I do like them. The
Queen Mum's my favourite actually.
NB: Why are they important to you?
Jim: Well, let's put it like this. They bring a lot of money
into the country and we can do with a few bob lately.

NB: But it's more than that though, surely?

Jim: Oh, it's a lot more than that. It's prestige, isn't it? There's nothing else like it, is there? You look at America. All they get is actors for presidents and things like that. No one goes to see them, do they?

NB: Why do you think tourists want to come and see all that?

Jim: Because they've got nothing like it over there, have they? All they've got is Roy Rogers and Trigger . . .

NB: Yes, well I must say, I'm not really a great royal fan.

Jim: I had gathered *that*, actually.

NB: I have a fondness for the Queen, but it's really the fondness you have for any familiar thing, I mean, like digestive biscuits and red pillar boxes. I wouldn't want her to go any more than I would want my old primary school to be knocked down, because anything you're familiar with that goes, it's part of your own identity going. But to me the royal family are part of my identity in that way and not in any other.

Jim: I think the royal family give a lot of people a lot of enjoyment, especially the older folk, people like that . . . they love it. It's just tradition, just tradition it is, and you know they like to see it.

Jim Batchelor, though my guide and informant, was baffled by our journey all over England in that it had brought him no check-list of characteristics that he could define as essentially and exclusively English. *Englishness* seemed to have treacherously eluded him.

NB: So, Jim, we've been the length and the breadth of the country; what have you found out about being English?

Jim: Well, believe it or not, I'm totally confused – totally! I always thought the British and the English was English, but I've seen so many variations of it now. It's confusing.

NB: Isn't that the point, Jim, that just because we have
a word 'Englishness' it doesn't mean there's anything simple
out there that corresponds to it? So you might think
participating in the Church of England was part of
Englishness, yet others would tell you that only going to
church for weddings and funerals was the English way. You
could say waving Union Jacks a lot and supporting the
Queen was being English, yet others would tell you the
English don't make a fuss about these things.
Jim: But a few years ago, the Englishman was a typical
crank, if you want to put it like that. It was sort of like us now.
NB: An eccentric?
Jim: Yes, well basically that's what he is now, isn't it?
NB: Well, that's part of it too. Once you have assumed
an English identity, you can use anything to bolster it, so
the fact of all being different becomes part of *being English*.
To ask, 'What is Englishness?' is a bit like asking 'What is
the shape of an amoeba?' It keeps changing its shape. That's
how you know it's alive.
Jim: Well, I don't give a monkey's. I'm still proud to be
English.

Jim is quite right to be confused. 'Englishness' tends to assume
that place of birth, culture and racial identity are the same. This
would hold in a world where English people lived only in
England, married only other English people and raised English
children exclusively in England. The possibility of believing in
such a world is long gone. Possibly our Victorian forefathers still
could, which is why the English identity was not problematic to
them. Nowadays, as every immigration officer knows, to define
nationality is a nightmare. Of course, it is always possible to keep
categories intact by dividing the world into the English and the
'really' English, those people for whom all the old assumptions
still hold, such as taking the C. of E. for a mark of nationality
rather than a religion. This highlights another point: that Eng-

lishness is an elastic category that can be stretched or reduced at will. To understand it, it may be more important, at any one time, to see who is *excluded* rather than who is *included*.

This vagueness should not be seen as a criticism of the notion of Englishness. Its power lies in its ability to mobilize history, emotion and collective sentiment, and create an identity that feels real. It has to be ambiguous to work at all. As Jim's reaction shows, the fact that we are unable to define something does not imply that we will cease to be emotionally attached to it. Had this been the case, the Christian religion would have died out centuries ago.

Am I proud to be English too? To a certain degree, yes. But any anthropologist is a professional alien so, for me the English will always be simultaneously 'us' and 'them'.